D1523658

SMART
SKIING

S M A R T
SKIING

**Mental Training
for All Ages
and All Levels
of Skill**

Dennis J. Selder

Jossey-Bass Publishers
San Francisco

Jossey-Bass books and products are available through most bookstores. To contact Jossey-Bass directly, call (888) 378–2537, fax to (800) 605–2665, or visit our website at www.josseybass.com.

Substantial discounts on bulk quantities of Jossey-Bass books are available to corporations, professional associations, and other organizations. For details and discount information, contact the special sales department at Jossey-Bass.

For sales outside the United States, please contact your local Simon & Schuster International Office.

 Manufactured in the United States of America on Lyons Falls Turin Book. This paper is acid-free and 100 percent totally chlorine-free.

Library of Congress Cataloging-in-Publication Data

Selder, Dennis J.
    Smart skiing: mental training for all ages and all levels of skill/
by Dennis J. Selder.
        p. cm.
    Includes bibliographical references (p.) and index.
    ISBN 0-7879-4143-3 (alk. paper)
    1. Skis and skiing—Psychological aspects. 2. Skis and skiing—
Training. I. Title.
GV854.9.P75S45   1998
796.93—dc21   98-6860

HB Printing   10 9 8 7 6 5 4 3 2 1   FIRST EDITION

*To Fran, who never ceases
to provide the love, support,
and encouragement
that make life a joyous
experience.*

Contents

Smart Sport
Series Preface

Have you ever imagined performing your favorite sport without error, as effortlessly as the sport's greatest athletes?

Have you ever had a feeling of absolute self-confidence just before performing?

Have you ever set short-, medium-, and long-range goals relative to your sport performance . . . and fully expected to reach each one?

Did you ever have so much fun participating that you never wanted to stop?

Twenty-five years ago, most recreational, college, and even national-level athletes responded no to such questions. In fact, back in the 1970s, when questions like these were first being asked by sport psychologists around the country, athletes and their coaches often only shook their heads at such questions, usually amused.

Things have changed over the past quarter-century. Today, when such questions are asked of the full range of sport participants, from beginning athletes to world-class champions, the answers are usually yes.

> *Yes, I can imagine error-free, effortless performance.*
> *Yes, I've felt total self-confidence prior to sport performance.*
> *Yes, I've set, and expected to achieve, my personal sport performance goals.*
> *Yes, I've really experienced a great deal of enjoyment while participating in my sport.*

It seems that most of us who are involved in sport, and even a good share of nonparticipants, know about and have attempted various performance enhancement techniques that involve psychology. Knowledgeable sport coaches and sport psychologists refer to these techniques as *psychological skills training*, or simply *mental training*. But not everyone who can answer yes to these and other mental training questions necessarily reaches full potential in sport, gets the most enjoyment from sport, or even continues to rehearse and refine his or her mental training techniques. Why not?

The main reason is that most individuals below the elite level of competition do not practice their mental skills with the same consistency that they devote to their physical training. This results, unfortunately, in a great number of sport participants who know about mental training but are not sure how to go about it effectively or how to use it to improve their physical skills and enjoyment. Thus statements like those above might be extended as follows:

> *I can imagine error-free, effortless performance; however, I can't seem to make the images translate to my physical performance.*
> *I've felt total self-confidence prior to sport performance, only to find my self-assurance disappear as soon as I start participating.*
> *I've set, and expected to achieve, my personal sport performance goals; but after a few were achieved, I've been unable to reach the others.*
> *I've really experienced a great deal of enjoyment in my sport; yet when I feel like I'm not improving, the fun wears off.*

The book you hold in your hands is one in a series published by Jossey-Bass designed to bring sport-specific applied sport psychology books to a new level of trustworthiness and practicality. To begin with, the books in the Smart Sport Series are written by experts not only in the specific sport under discussion but also in applied sport psychology. Each of the books in the Smart Sport Series has a common backbone of content which ensures that the most important common elements of sport psychology are treated within each of the titles in the Series. Each covers the principles and practical aspects of achievement motivation, arousal regulation, psychological skills training, self-confidence, goal setting, concentration, and enjoyment that are pertinent to the sport under discussion. Other features are self-tests to help you evaluate your current status in a variety of sport psychology and mental skills areas. Special highlight boxes make it easy to comprehend and remember key points, and focused bibliographies help you find the most significant references on important topics.

Finally, each of the Series books is rich in examples to help you understand and internalize the principles that can lead you to a higher level of sport performance. This combination of expert writing, sport expertise, core psychological principles, and sport-specific examples helps to make the Smart Sport Series the smart choice for both male and female athletes of all ages and abilities who are looking to move to the next level of personal achievement.

Each book in the Smart Sport Series is a tool. For beginning athletes, it can serve as an enlightening introduction to a new sport. For veterans, it can repair faulty performance and improve on already solid technique and strategy. For everyone, it can help build a new model of sport-specific learning and personal understanding that can help achieve personal best performance. I encourage you to use this book to help find that peace of mind that comes from knowing you've done your best in sport to become the best you are capable of becoming!

RICK FREY, PH.D.
GENERAL EDITOR

Preface

Skiing can be an experience in exhilaration, excitement, serenity, and inner peace. It can also be scary, intimidating, frustrating, and boring. Why isn't skiing a positive adventure for most of us a majority of the time? The answer lies in the way each of us interprets our world. Some of us are defeated, or at least distracted, by obstacles and challenges that push us past our comfort level. Others thrive on such obstacles, using the energy it takes to overcome them to power upward to new levels of achievement and personal satisfaction. Because each of us is unique, we look at life a little differently. If you want to look at your skiing in a more positive light, orienting your mountain experiences toward better performance and greater enjoyment and away from fear and anxiety, you'll find this book valuable.

After years of working with many skiers, from raw beginners to international competitors, I believe that skiing can lead to positive, peak experiences for *anyone*. Beginning, intermediate, or advanced skier, teenager or senior, male or female, you can influence your psychological health and well-being by becoming a smart skier—that is, by taking control of your skiing through the use of proven motivation, learning, and performance principles from the exciting field of sport psychology.

The knowledge base in the field of applied sport psychology has grown exponentially over the past thirty years. Unfortunately, this information has primarily been accessible only to professional sport psychologists, who possess the interest, education, and training to read professional journals and books. For the most part, the general public has been left in the dark about sport psychology and how to apply its principles.

Since 1962, I've been studying sport and sport psychology. While educating athletes from a variety of sports, of all ages and backgrounds, in groups and one-on-one, I've tried to show them how to use their sport to become more effective human beings and how to become better athletes in the process. Sport psychology techniques are being made available to client-athletes by sport psychologists like me every day, but little of this information is presented to the public in a manner that can be understood or applied. It's time for a change. I wrote this book so that any skier can read and understand the same principles that have been applied to helping our Olympic and professional athletes perform to the best of their abilities. I hope it will teach you that through understanding simple principles governing thinking and behaving, you can influence your motivation, learning, and performance (the critical factors in any human endeavor). You'll also learn effective applied sport psychology strategies that can easily be applied to your skiing.

I've organized this book using the same methods that I've found helpful in educating athletes over the past thirty years. As a sport psychology consultant, my job is to identify the source of a problem that an athlete is experiencing and then to design an intervention that helps solve the problem. Under normal circumstances, the athlete needs to practice and eventually learn new psychological skills. Unless athletes are convinced that the intervention will work, however, they will not practice the new mental skills that will help them. It became evident to me early in my professional career that athletes accepted interventions only when they understood the way information was processed, the value of setting priorities and planning, and the role of anxiety, arousal, and attention on concentration. In short, each athlete needed a crash course in how humans think and behave. This approach has proven very successful over the years, helping athletes of all abilities move to the next or higher levels of performance.

If you understand how you think and behave, you can solve problems and figure out what's happening to you in sport. Methods you use to overcome problems become meaningful and personal. Chapter One covers the critical principles governing thinking and behaving. It includes descriptions of the personality characteristics that can affect how you learn and perform in skiing and an assessment designed to help you determine which of these characteristics best describe you. In Chapter Two, we take a look at how to establish personal performance goals in skiing so that you can achieve your most important outcomes and keep your motivation high. In Chapter Three, we explore the learning principles that underlie getting the most from both your formal instruction and your skiing experiences. Chapter Four integrates principles of performance with what you have learned in Chapter One about your personal characteristics to help you achieve a consistently high level of performance. The next two chapters cover the proven mental skills associated with skiing competence. In Chapter Five, we discuss the emotional control skills that can lead to peak experiences in skiing, particularly such skills as progressive muscular relaxation, which are designed to handle anxiety and fear. Chapter Six covers additional mental skills, particularly the use of imagery and attention control skills. Chapter Seven discusses the relationship between increased skiing confidence and enjoyment and provides concrete suggestions for integrating your skiing experiences with the techniques and skills presented throughout the book. At the end of the book you'll also find two handy appendixes: Appendix A provides goal-setting forms that you can use to help you determine, set, follow, and evaluate your ski-related goals; Appendix B is a list of selected skiing references.

I've had a passion for skiing since the late 1950s. This passion still burns strongly and gets me skiing as often as my university and consulting schedules allow. My wife and four children also ski. Our experience as a family skiing together is priceless and continues to enrich our lives. I've been fortunate to serve as a consultant for the Mammoth Mountain downhill racing program for eight years and have had experience consulting with international-level skiers.

What I have observed as both a skier and a sport psychologist is that people of all ages and abilities continually strive to improve their skiing. Whether people ski a couple of times a year or are members of a World Cup team, they want to make each run better. Improvement translates into more satisfaction, fun, and enjoyment for skiers of all abilities.

The best way to improve is by learning how to get the most from your skiing experiences. Smart skiers want to discover everything they can about themselves and their sport and to apply that knowledge effectively. *Smart Skiing* can help you gain insight about yourself as a person and, in the process, help you become a much better skier. I wish you good luck in your quest . . . and good skiing!

San Diego, California
July 1998

DENNIS J. SELDER

Acknowledgments

I would like to acknowledge the essential contributions of many individuals who have made this book possible. The series editor, Rick Frey, has been a great help in the production of the manuscript. He has been a constant source of creative professional expertise, constructive criticism, and support. I also owe a debt to the many skiers and ski coaches at Mammoth Mountain and to Kevin Burnett at Mount Bachelor, Noel Duftey at Heavenly Valley, Daryl Whittaker at Kirkwood, and Robert Weyms, now in Switzerland, for their expertise on skiing performance, coaching, and instruction. I also thank my best critic, Fran, and my kids, without whose support and willingness to go skiing this book would not have been possible.

Acknowledgments

SMART

SKIING

1

Understanding Yourself and Smart Skiing

 *We barely have time to step into our skis after getting off the gondola at the top of the mountain. I have been invited to ski with a group of experienced ski coaches and expert ski racers, and, believe me, I am not in their class. They take off with great exuberance—right over a ledge! I follow despite the fact that I can't even see over it. I know that the mountainside below me is incredibly steep. My adrenaline is pumping. Scared? You bet!*

I follow one of the experts as he takes an angle along the lip of the ledge. Then he disappears into space! I want to stop, to analyze the situation, but I have made a bet with myself on this run: without fear or overanalysis getting in the way, I'm going to trust my body to ski.

I hit the lip and am airborne. I see the steepness of the line below me. Things are moving too fast for me to be afraid. I land under control and begin picking up speed. Too much speed! At this point everything I'd said to myself on the gondola about staying calm and focused is overcome by unmistakable fear. My body is tense and barely able to respond. I need to regain control. Somehow I manage to make a turn and come to a stop in the middle of the narrow chute that my expert friends are just completing below. I catch my breath and wonder if I can sidestep my way off this tortuous face. Then I notice my friends standing together looking back up at me. I experience an uncomfortable feeling. I am on the steepest, most difficult run of my skiing career, gripped by the powerful knowledge that if I fall on this run, I might not only tumble in a mass of flailing skis, poles, and broken bones but also not even survive. Yet hundreds of feet below me are coaches and racers I've worked with to improve their own control over self-doubt, fear, anger, and other emotions that cripple top performance. I imagine that each of them is wondering if I practice what I preach.

I am aware that the physical tools I need to get off this mountain are inside me, that the only thing I need is the confidence to use them. Almost immediately I hear a sarcastic voice in my head that ridicules this notion, reminding me that I've never been on a mountain this steep, that I'm a university sport psychologist who should know better than to think he can ski with expert racers over such difficult terrain. I stand there wrestling with these two opposite thoughts. One is positive and hopeful, the other negative and fearful. For a few moments I am actually paralyzed by confusion.

And that's when a marvelous thing happens. I see my friends far below signaling for me to continue. I can't hear them shouting, but I know they are encouraging and urging me to go for it. I feel some confidence return. It's the confidence that I have another set of tools, mental training techniques, that can help me find my physical skills. As I exhale, the upper part of my body begins to relax, and I sense energy and power filtering into my legs. My attention is directed to the fall line as my skis turn downhill.

After the first turn, I sense how wonderful the snow conditions are. Feeling the light powder relaxes me, and I get into the run. Pure joy completely replaces abject fear. I have one of those runs that a skier can never forget. I am flying down the mountain, my body on automatic pilot. I am in total control of my environment. Although I am moving at high speed, everything seems to be in slow motion. I see the rocks, trees, and moguls clearly, and I have more time than usual to make decisions about weighting, edges, and direction. Suddenly—surprisingly—I am skidding to a stop among my companions.

They stand there smiling and nodding. One of them says, "Wow!" I can't speak, but I feel free and somehow different. As a sport psychologist, I know that I've just had what is referred to as a peak experience. As a skier, I know that I want to keep this feeling forever.

What is it that causes some people to change their lives and thoughts once enough snow has fallen on their favorite mountain? Why is it that some take to skis like a duck to water, whereas others struggle for years to develop basic skills? How can you get the most out of your skiing experiences? What is the best way to develop high-level skill that will allow you to ski those double diamond runs with confidence? How do you handle fear, frustration, and discouragement on the mountain?

The answers to these and other skiing-related questions are based on a very personal kind of knowledge. To make real progress in skiing or in any other endeavor, you need to know and understand yourself. The methods for obtaining this knowledge have been available to sport psychologists for years, and I am going to share them with you.

My plan for doing so is fairly simple. I am going to help you develop a better understanding of how your body responds to experiences, and then I will relate that knowledge to learning how to ski and skiing performance. This approach will not only help you gain general insight into learning and performance but also help you understand how this information can directly affect your skiing experiences. Each piece of knowledge will build a clearer understanding of just what exactly is happening when you ski down the mountain and how you can change that experience if you wish.

Understanding Yourself

In order to realize your potential as a skier, you need to understand who you are and how you operate as a skier. None of us goes through life in a vacuum. We all possess some knowledge about ourselves. Generally, however, we have a large amount of uncertainty about what we are capable of, how we'll respond to stressors, and what we'll do in certain situations. We often seek either reinforcement or clarification of what we believe about ourselves. In the following pages you'll have ample opportunities to find out more about yourself and how you can apply this self-knowledge to your skiing.

Once you gain accurate information about how you are motivated, how you learn, and how you concentrate under pressure, you can then apply the knowledge in a personalized way to improve your skiing performance and enjoyment. This journey will at first seem somewhat intimidating. Once you've gone through this process of increasing your self-awareness, however, you'll possess the insights necessary to employ specific mental training techniques to great advantage in enhancing your performance and skiing experiences. Remember also that you can apply the same concepts and principles to other endeavors in your life.

Have you ever watched an accomplished skier traverse a thrilling double diamond run? Have you ever hoped that some day you could sail down that kind of terrain with the same grace and poise? You don't necessarily have to wait. Peak experiences are not the exclusive property of advanced skiers, and that is the real beauty of skiing. You can have a peak experience any time you encounter a good match between your knowledge and skills and the challenges presented by the mountain, regardless of the difficulty rating of the slope.

> You can have a peak experience any time you encounter a good match between your knowledge and skills and the challenges presented by the mountain.

Your body is fantastic, and your brain, with more than 250 billion cells, is the master control of your behavior. You're able to assimilate and store unlimited information, and use it when you need it. You can control more than seven hundred muscles working in

unison to accomplish a task. All your body systems—
nervous system, muscular system, circulatory system,
and so on—function together when you're skiing. Skiing to the best of your ability can be achieved by allow-
ing your body to respond. The key is not letting your
thoughts interfere with your performance. Skilled motor performance, which occurs quickly in skiing, can-
not happen if you are thinking while you are moving.
Once you have decided what to do, you let your body
go on automatic pilot.

Sport skills like skiing are complex movement patterns that take considerable time and effort to learn. It
does not matter how old you are or how coordinated
you think yourself to be. It's possible to learn how to
ski and to ski well. One of the great characteristics of
skiing is that it continually
challenges the skier, from the
beginner to the world-class
athlete. The real beauty of
skiing is that it can enhance
our quality of life: we may
get a thrill from the challenge,
the speed and excitement, the

> Being aware of what motivates you can help you achieve personal skiing expression and fulfillment.

fear, the solitude, and the beauty of the surroundings; or we may be thrilled hearing the hum of the ski
lift as we pass through a stand of large evergreens,
enjoying the camaraderie of our ski group, or feeling

the satisfaction that comes from accomplishment. Being aware of what motivates you can help you achieve personal skiing expression and fulfillment.

Personality, Concentration, and Skiing

Your personality and ability to concentrate strongly affect how you make decisions. Because of their crucial role in your decision making, we should take some time to better understand personality and concentration. Your personality controls how you perceive what is happening both inside your body and in the immediate outside environment. Your concentration abilities influence how well you are able to focus on internal and external events at any point in time. Let's explore the critical aspects of personality and concentration that control personal decision making by studying an illustration. Figure 1.1 is a graphic representation of how personality affects skiing performance, learning, and skiing enjoyment.

Your personality core represents the real you. It's the central part of you as a unique person. Your core is thought to be the most powerful influence on making the kinds of decisions that are of importance to you. The more important a question or issue, the more involved your core becomes. For example, an easy question that

Figure 1.1
Relationship Between Personality and Skiing Performance,
Learning, and Enjoyment

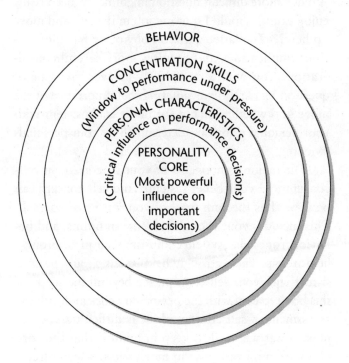

BEHAVIOR

CONCENTRATION SKILLS
(Window to performance under pressure)

PERSONAL CHARACTERISTICS
(Critical influence on performance decisions)

PERSONALITY
CORE
(Most powerful
influence on
important
decisions)

wouldn't necessarily involve your personality core might be, "Do I want to ski chair five or chair three?" A much more difficult question might be, "Since I really enjoy skiing, should I quit my job in the city and move up here?" The latter question obviously has more serious implications and requires more careful consideration. You would most likely answer this type of question by carefully evaluating the importance of the move and whether or not the move is consistent with your personal priorities (determined by your personality core).

The major components of your core are your self-concept and your belief system. Your self-concept can be viewed as the sum total of your views of yourself. This includes your thoughts, ideas, emotions, and behavior. Your belief system comprises your most strongly held beliefs. These strongly held beliefs should be consistent with your self-concept. It's beyond the scope of this book to deal with the personality core in detail; the assessment of self-concept alone is difficult and complex. What we need to keep in mind is that the core plays an important role in motivation, which affects how we pursue our goals. For most of us, our decisions about what we want to achieve in skiing are important ones, as they will involve significant amounts of time, energy, and money. In Chapter Two we'll examine the components of your core so that you can prioritize your top three skiing outcomes or long-range goals.

As you go out from the center in Figure 1.1, the next concentric circle represents your personal characteristics. These characteristics are integrated with, and complementary to, your personality core in making decisions. Your core is the primary influence over important personal decisions. The less important the decision, the more influential your personal characteristics become. These personal characteristics are not as stable over time as your personality core, but they are intimately associated with daily decisions. The characteristics selected for inclusion in this book were chosen because of their influence on personal perceptions of stress. Why? Because anxiety (part of the stress response) caused by perceived stressors is the number-one reason why individuals don't reach their full potential in skiing. Anxiety is also the number-one reason why a person's enjoyment in skiing may fall short. As you'll see in the following chapters, perceptions of stress actually cause mental problems with your ability to perform, especially under conditions of high stress. Under such conditions, you end up getting distracted, limiting your ability to respond both physically and mentally. These types of distractions, delays, and mistakes can cause individuals to slip into downward performance spirals that can ultimately lead to choking.

Conversely, you'll also discover that you can learn to use coping strategies and mental skills to alter your perceptions and control your anxiety responses. It is well known in elite sport and throughout the field of sport psychology that individuals who are able to maintain concentration under a wide variety of stressful performance conditions are the ones who consistently achieve the highest levels of performance.

Using a brief assessment at the end of this chapter, you'll be able to identify your most dominant personal characteristics. Armed with this new self-awareness, you will be able to identify possible sources of anxiety related to your skiing and thus to plan so as to avoid the disrupting effects of anxiety on your performance.

Directly related to your personal characteristics is your ability to concentrate effectively. You can think of your concentration skills as a window into your performance under stress. Skiing is a complex sport requiring quick decision making under extreme time demands. For example, if you're traveling at a high rate of speed and you suddenly sense a bump, it's too late to respond. It takes about 225 milliseconds (or 0.225 second) to respond to a signal. Traveling at a relatively slow rate of speed for skiing, say fifteen miles per hour, you'll have traveled almost five feet by the time you decide what to do. Skiing requires you to anticipate in advance of the actual performance of a skill.

Skillful skiing requires well-developed attention skills. Back in 1976, sport psychologist Robert Nideffer explained that in any kind of human activity, we constantly need to direct our focus of attention in two major dimensions: width and location. At any given moment, our attention is either narrow or broad (width) and either internal or external (location) relative to our body. Our approach in this book is that all concentration skills in skiing can be determined by (1) your ability to scan a lot of information, both inside your body and in the environment; and (2) your ability to narrow your concentration on one factor and ignore everything else, sometimes under intense pressure. Not only are each of these skills important, but you have to be able to switch your focus of attention depending on the demands of the situation. If your concentration skills match the demands of a given situation, and you have the knowledge (both cognitive and motor) to respond, you will achieve smooth coordinated motor performance. The coordination of attention, knowledge, and physical skill is what leads individuals to have peak experiences, or joyous feelings of "flow," while skiing.

> Individuals who are able to maintain concentration under a wide variety of stressful performance conditions are the ones who consistently achieve the highest levels of performance.

Making effective decisions has implications for your ability to learn as well as for your performance in a particular situation. (We'll talk more about learning and how it is differentiated from performance in Chapters Three and Four.) In learning how to ski, the most important mental ability is your capacity to focus your attention on the correct learning cue. If you know what cue to focus on and have the ability to focus correctly, your learning will progress quickly and efficiently. If you don't use effective attention control skills, learning occurs by chance and much more slowly. The processes of effective ski-related learning are discussed in detail in Chapter Three.

The assessment section at the end of this chapter asks you to rate your concentration skills. This assessment will give you insight into how you normally handle the concentration demands of skiing. Your knowledge of your concentration skills and of your dominant personal characteristics (also derived from the assessment) will enable you to identify what generally causes you to be distracted or causes you mental and physical problems as your perceptions of anxiety increase. Figure 1.2 illustrates the relationship between stressors, perception, and performance.

Notice in Figure 1.2 that whether your skiing performance is optimal or miserable (that is, you choke) depends on how you perceive stressors in your internal environment (cues coming from inside your body) or your external environment (cues coming from outside your body). As an example, assume that you're standing at the top of a run that you've never skied before. You perceive that the hill is too steep and that

Figure 1.2
Relationship Between Stressors, Perception, and Performance

Skiing Stressor

↓

Skier Perception of Stressor

High Performance Responses

Arousal is optimal.
Attention focus is on task-relevant cues.
Muscles are relaxed and ready to respond.

Performance Problem Responses

Arousal is too high/low.
Attention focus is not on task-relevant cues.
Muscles are not ready to respond.

High-Level Performance

• Skiing without thought
• Body responding to challenges
• Feelings of control and exhilaration

Performance Problems

• Missed cues
• Response too quick or too slow
• Loss of emotional control

Skiing "in the zone"

Performance Continuum

Choking

it's going to require you to ski with skill you don't possess. What happens?

One possibility is that you become very frightened and find yourself unable to move. In this scenario you might say to yourself, "There is no way I can ski this run. I'll really get hurt if I even try." Another possibility is that you look at the same run and say to yourself, "This is steeper than anything I've ever skied, but I can ski this slope because I can stop anytime I please if it gets too demanding. I can also traverse my way down if I get into difficulty."

In this example, two different perceptions result from the same stressor (in this case, hill steepness). The different perceptions are primarily caused by how you interpret the stressor. Your interpretation is controlled by your dominant personal characteristics. In later chapters you'll learn to interpret environmental and internal stressors in ways that can help you make positive skiing decisions. Chapter Four explains how to focus your attention under pressure; Chapters Five and Six provide detailed information about how to learn emotional control and concentration skills that will help you perform under a variety of pressures.

Personal Assessments

I mentioned Bob Nideffer earlier. Bob is a psychologist who has been instrumental in applying knowledge from clinical psychology to sport environments. The assessments of concentration and personal characteristics presented here are based on his earlier work.

It's important for you to identify which of the following personal characteristics are most descriptive of you, because your dominant characteristics determine what kinds of stressors related to skiing cause you anxiety. Once you have identified what causes you to become anxious, you can then plan how to overcome the tendency to become anxious.

It's also possible that you have general characteristics that represent how you behave most of the time but that may or may not be true when you're skiing. If you have *concentration* errors in skiing and these are not characteristic of you generally, then use skiing as a specific application in rating your concentration and personal characteristics. If you generally operate better skiing, and it is other life situations that cause you stress, then take a general approach to the ratings. You'll be asked to rate your concentration skills first and then your personal characteristics.

Concentration Skills Assessment

The following aspects of concentration relate to your ability to direct your focus of attention. Understanding your strengths and weaknesses with regard to these characteristics of attention control can guide you in the improvement exercises presented later.

Broad Focus of Attention

Rate yourself high on this skill if you're able to take in information from a variety of sources. You are confident handling a lot of things going on at the same time and are able to think about them clearly. You're good at interpreting your environment and analyzing this information internally. If either or both of these characteristics describe you very well, rate yourself high (10 is the highest). If either or both are only sometimes descriptive of you, give yourself a 5. If these abilities don't describe you at all, rate yourself a 1.

Your rating: _____

Narrow Focus of Attention

If you can focus your attention, and filter or block distractions, rate yourself high (10 is the highest). If you're easily distracted, rate yourself lower (1 is the lowest).

Your rating: _____

Personal Characteristics Assessment

The following characteristics have been identified as related to anxiety. If you can identify the characteristic that best describes you, then you're well on your way to controlling anxiety. As before, you'll be asked to rate yourself on a scale of 1 to 10. A rating of 1 means that in no way does this characteristic describe you, a 5 means that some of the time it describes you, and a 10 means that it always describes you. After you go through each of the personal characteristics, you need to determine which among all the top-rated characteristics are most descriptive of you. Later, in Chapter Four, I'll explain what you can do to reduce the interfering effects of anxiety.

List Person vs. Let-It-Happen Person

The list person is the type who wakes up in the morning and goes to his or her list. If the day proceeds and the list is taken care of, such an individual would rate the day a success. If this is absolutely descriptive of you, rate yourself a 10. If this is not descriptive of you, give yourself a score of 1.

Your rating: _____

If you would rather wake up in the morning and look forward to a day of challenges (the more the better), and you feel that you have the energy to take care of anything that happens, you're a let-it-happen person. Rate yourself on a scale of 1 to 10, 1 being not descriptive and 10 being absolutely descriptive.

Your rating: _____

Socially Controlled vs. Socially Autonomous Person

The socially controlled individual always knows and acts the way a responsible member of society is expected to act, no matter what the situation may be. Rate yourself on a scale of 1 to 10, where 1 indicates that you're not socially controlled and 10 means that this characteristic describes you very well.

Your rating: _____

The opposite of the socially controlled person is the individual who knows exactly how he or she should behavē but really doesn't care what anyone else or society thinks of his or her behavior. Rate yourself on social autonomy on a scale of 1 to 10. If you're a strongly socially autonomous person give yourself a 10. If you're definitely not this type of person, give yourself a 1.

Your rating: _____

Superperson vs. Cautious Person

Superpersons are self-confident, have a high need to control what is going on, and set very high standards. It is the combination of these factors that make individuals superpersons. If this describes you well, rate yourself a 10. If it definitely does not describe you, give yourself a 1.

Your rating: _____

If you have a tendency to look to others to determine what you should be doing, if you personalize criticism, and if you set safe goals, give yourself a 10 for caution on the rating scale. If this does not describe you in the least, give yourself a 1.

Your rating: _____

Slow vs. Fast Decision Maker

If you have a definite tendency to analyze things and worry about them, and have difficulty taking action, you can rate yourself high on the slow decision maker scale. If this tendency is not part of your personality, give yourself 1.

Your rating: _____

If you're the type of person who makes decisions very quickly and confidently, give yourself a 10 for fast decision making.

Your rating: _____

Silence Is Golden vs. Stream of Consciousness Person

Individuals express themselves in different ways. In this category, pick the one description that fits you best and give it a rating on a 10-point scale. The first type is the individual who easily expresses thoughts, and the thoughts are generally positive.

Your rating: _____

The second type is the individual who expresses thoughts easily, but the thoughts are generally critical. The critical expression may include anger.

Your rating: _____

The third type is the person who has a definite tendency to keep quiet but who analyzes things in a positive way.

Your rating: _____

The fourth type is the individual who hesitates to express himself or herself but who analyzes things in a critical manner.

Your rating: _____

Determine which characteristics are most descriptive of you. You may have rated yourself high in more than one category. If you rated yourself a 4, 5, or 6 in all categories, you still need to determine what is most characteristic of you. Check with someone who knows you well. If they agree with you, your assessment is probably accurate. If they don't agree with you, check with other individuals who know you well. Take the consensus as the most accurate. It is crucial that you make this determination because, though it may seem ironic, when you're operating under pressure it is often your dominant characteristic that causes you to become distracted.

Identifying your relative strengths enables you to plan solutions to your concentration problems. Under pressure, we tend to go with what we are best at. So if, for example, my dominant descriptor is that of superperson, I can look to this characteristic as a major source of anxiety, particularly when I am under pressure. I can verify this by looking at the kinds of experiences I have had in the past. Do I get upset when I don't accomplish what I intended? Does it bother me when I don't know what is causing my mistakes? These are examples of common experiences that cause anxiety for the superperson. If this is my dominant personal characteristic, it would thus be prudent for me to look after these sources of anxiety first. Later, I may wish to go back and attack another source of anxiety.

As I mentioned earlier, in Chapter Four we'll use your ratings to help you determine what events and thoughts in skiing will most likely cause you anxiety. We will also refer to your top-rated personal characteristics in the next chapter, where we will discuss motivation and work to determine your appropriate long-range outcomes and shorter-term performance goals. Please write your three top personal characteristics and their associated ratings here:

Three Top Characteristics   **Rating**

1. _____   _____

2. _____   _____

3. _____   _____

This chapter has introduced you to *Smart Skiing*'s theme of personal insight. Through an understanding of your own personal characteristics, you can develop significant control over how motivated you are, how well you learn, and how well you can perform on any given day. In the next chapter we'll consider in more detail the fascinating subject of motivation. Motivation is our first in-depth area of exploration because no matter what level of skier you are, when you're properly motivated you'll spend more time accomplishing what is important to you. This translates into more personal gratification and enjoyment from your skiing experiences.

2

Motivated Skiing

 *Before the downhill season, Mary and her coach set realistic performance goals. Their ultimate goal for the season was to make the region's top five list. She reached the goal a little past halfway* through the season, held onto the ranking for the balance of the year, and ended up ranked third overall. Because of her ranking, she had been invited to the regional championships. Now, the championships over, she stood at the bottom of the hill with her coach, evaluating her performance.

Both of her downhill runs in the championships had been disasters. She'd missed gates on both runs and had been disqualified. A feeling of disappointment enveloped her. "I don't know, Coach. I just didn't have it today. I thought I was ready, but I guess I wasn't."

The coach nodded in agreement. "You weren't prepared for championship performance today," he said. "You didn't have your usual drive to win. And I think I know why."

Mary looked up at him, surprised. "You do?"

"We failed to prepare for the championships, and that set us up for failure. Your goal this year was to make the top five; once you achieved your goal, you no longer had a reason for continuing to improve your performance. We should have adjusted your season's ultimate goal when it looked certain that you would earn a place at the championships. Though the championship races were difficult, they were well within your ability to win. Your initial success made it seem like your season was over too early."

Mary looked down, embarrassed and saddened. The coach put his arm around her. "We'll both know better next year," he said with a smile. She slowly looked up from the snow, and a smile spread across her face as well.

Not much gets done without motivation, and nothing motivates like difficult yet reachable goals. In this chapter we'll look at how you can best plan your own motivational strategies to move toward your long-range outcomes by setting shorter-term performance goals. The chapter begins with an overview of how motivation relates to you and your goals. We then discuss how to determine your outcomes and set goals. Finally, using the example of a typical intermediate skier, we look at a set of performance goals chosen to achieve this skier's desired outcome. As you read through this chapter, I encourage you to think about and write down outcomes and goals that seem appropriate for you. You can use the goal-setting form in Appendix A for this purpose.

Motivated Behavior

As we begin, let's get one thing straight about what I mean by *motivation*. We can be stimulated to start an activity through the persuasion of individuals, groups, or advertising campaigns. This kind of motivation comes from outside sources and is not under our personal control. We are talking about a different kind of motivation in this book—the kind that comes from within each of us, the kind that gives us control over our own behavior.

Your motivation for skiing comes from your personality core, from who you are as a person. This central core drives your thinking about what is important to you, how intense you'll become, and what effort you are willing to expend. You make your decisions—about whether to begin skiing, whether to continue skiing, and how intense your skiing can be—in a rational manner. Knowing what is important to you and understanding motivation can help you make more rational decisions.

Your personality, formed by a combination of your life experiences and your genetic makeup, is what makes you unique from others. You can think of your personality simply as the sum total of your personal characteristics. We will discuss those characteristics that have a direct influence on how you are motivated.

Competitive Drive

The need to be competitive relates not only to dominating another person or group but also to the pressure we put on ourselves to excel and be competent. The greater our competitive drive, the more important it becomes to master the skills necessary to excel. Skiers high in competitive drive define excellence not only in terms of racing against others but also in terms of developing the necessary skills to ski competently relative to their own standards of excellence.

Many skiers judge their skiing solely on how much they improve after each run or after each ski trip. These skiers often feel frustrated if their skiing ability does not reflect their expected level of competence. As we'll soon see, you need to set your skiing goals in a way that reflects reality. It's unlikely that a person can become an elite skier by skiing only two weeks each year. It's a bit more realistic for a two-week skier to focus on one aspect of improved skiing—for example, learning the proper techniques for taking air (that is, leaving the snow surface, becoming airborne, for brief periods of time). You experience great satisfaction when you achieve realistic goals. Smart skiers set realistic goals and experience satisfaction, as opposed to frustration and discouragement.

Competitive drive comprises both comparing yourself to others and achieving personal development goals. If you're a competition skier, each race provides you plentiful opportunities for comparison. For the rest of us, it's much tougher to get satisfaction, because we tend to compare ourselves to people who ski better than we do. Such comparisons rarely allow us to succeed. Smart skiers don't set themselves up for failure.

> Smart skiers set realistic goals and experience satisfaction, as opposed to frustration and discouragement.

Competing only with yourself leads to the greatest satisfaction and sustained motivation. You can't control how well others ski, but you can control your own performance. Set your goals to improve your own skiing technique. Your feelings of improvement and development as a skier will increase your satisfaction and motivation.

Self-Confidence

Your self-confidence and competitiveness both strongly influence the nature and difficulty of the goals you set. For example, if you're self-confident and competitive, you'll set difficult goals for yourself. If you lack self-confidence or have a low competitive drive, your goals will be less rigorous, with correspondingly lower standards of performance.

Self-confident individuals tend to become frustrated because they often fail to attain their more difficult goals. Less confident individuals achieve their goals but are likewise dissatisfied because they often realize they could have done much better. If you're smart about the goals you set, you decrease your chances of becoming frustrated; it's very important to consider your level of self-confidence when setting goals.

Self-confidence also relates to staying motivated. Once we start skiing, we get feedback, and how we interpret the feedback helps determine how motivated we stay. Individuals high in self-confidence tend to interpret feedback in a positive light, even if the feedback is critical, because they perceive the feedback as related to competence. Individuals low in self-confidence tend to take critical feedback personally, which reduces their motivation. If you are low in self-confidence, remind yourself to use critical feedback to improve your skiing, not to put yourself down. Although you may struggle with this process your whole life, being objective about feedback will become more automatic with time.

Need for Control

Your need to be in control of your life also influences your motivation. If you have a strong need for self-determination, setting precise goals will be important to you. If you actually prefer being told what to do, you'll actively seek others to set goals for you. From a mental health perspective, it's much better to be involved in your own goal setting.

Expression

A young woman lying in the snow crying and smashing her pole against a mogul is demonstrating clear *expression* of her thoughts. The way we interpret what is happening to us and the way we express ourselves influences our motivation. We can divide the ways we express ourselves into two main categories: being critical and being positive.

Some individuals have a decided tendency to be critical. After just completing a run or attempting a new skill, critical persons usually analyze what happened in a negative way—that is, they dwell on what went wrong. At times this can be a helpful characteristic, because by constantly detecting mistakes, the critical person increases the chances that they will correct the errors. Unfortunately, this kind of negativity can lead to a lot of unnecessary anxiety and interference with learning and performance. For example, the young woman in the snow may have been trying to master mogul skiing when she became completely frustrated. Her behavior then prevents her from achieving her original objective of improved mogul skiing because it leads her to ask questions unrelated to performance: whether or not to get back up, whether she should quit skiing, and so on.

The opposite of self-criticism is self-promotion, which is the tendency to be positive when analyzing what has just happened. The strength of this characteristic is that you'll not become burdened or overloaded by your mistakes but will instead maintain a positive attitude. The weakness of the self-promotion approach is that you may not recognize, and therefore not correct, your mistakes.

You can avoid the negative aspects of either characteristic by objectively analyzing both positive and negative aspects of a performance. You will thus be able to recognize the progress you're making while still decreasing the number of errors you commit.

Decision-Making Style

If you are generally a confident person who makes decisions quickly, the influence of your decision-making style on motivation is generally positive; it will help you work toward difficult and challenging goals. My one warning regarding this style of behavior is that you may make decisions too quickly. As we see later in this chapter, making hasty decisions has many implications for setting outcomes (what you want to gain from your skiing experiences). By taking the time to discuss your plans with others, you can often avoid frustration.

If you have a tendency to delay decisions and think about them for some time, the implications for motivation are more direct. It is typically tougher for slow decision makers to make a commitment to skiing. The recommendations later in the chapter regarding setting challenging and realistic goals are of considerable importance if you want to enjoy your skiing experiences to the fullest.

Socialization

Because our personality is influenced by our experiences, we need to look briefly at *socialization*, the process by which society establishes its standards. Society can influence our decision making in ways that may or may not be consistent with our personal core.

As a way of illustrating the socialization process, consider the following contrasting "norms" for competitiveness. Up until a few years ago, North American society socialized women to believe that it was not feminine to be highly competitive. At the same time, men were socialized to believe that to be a man you needed to be competitive. You may have grown up in an environment that accepted such stereotypes.

Socialization may have little to do with who you actually are. Clinical psychologists tell us that acting in ways that contradict your personality causes stress. Because stress creates illness, failing to express your true nature is counterproductive to your health and enjoyment of skiing.

To return to our example, not only are females competitive, but careful scientific studies have demonstrated that elite female athletes are often more competitive than their male counterparts. Being competitive is part of who we are, and to repress or exaggerate this characteristic only creates stress. Competition in its healthiest form is one of the joys in living. Healthy competition is available to each of us: all we have to do is set meaningful personal goals and work to achieve them. If we base our goals on our true self and not on outside influences, we can ensure our success. Unfortunately, parents and coaches sometimes forget that motivation is under the control of the person being motivated. For best results, your motivation should be under your direct control: you need to know exactly what you're doing, why you're doing it, and how you're going to measure your efforts.

Outcomes, Goals, and Motivation

Your *outcome* is what you are attempting to achieve in the long run. To achieve your outcome you need to set specific, measurable performance goals, and you need to understand how much time and effort will be needed to achieve those goals. You will be more motivated if you place a high degree of importance on the outcome, if you are certain that your performance goals will achieve your outcome, and if you are certain that the effort you expend will lead to achievement of your performance goals. Seeing that the effort and energy you direct toward measurable goals actually results in success is what will maintain and stimulate your motivation. Figure 2.1 illustrates these relationships. I hasten to point out that it is the *direction* of the motivation in Figure 2.1 that is important, not the angle of the slope. In other words, there are no scientific studies verifying that one unit of certainty equals one unit of motivation. However, there is a general pattern: motivation increases with increasing outcome importance, performance goal certainty, and effort certainty. Each time you see yourself reach a performance goal, it becomes evident that you are closer to achieving your outcome,

> Healthy competition is available to each of us: all we have to do is set meaningful personal goals and work to achieve them.

and you become even more motivated in your behavior.

In the next section, we will look at how your core personality and characteristics influence your priorities and thus your desired outcomes. With a good understanding of your priorities, you can set effective goals. I recommend that you review Figure 1.1 and the accompanying discussion in Chapter One before reading on.

Determining Your Desired Outcomes

The best way to establish your most important priorities is to take a look at who you are and what you're about. In psychological terms, your self-concept and belief systems—how you perceive yourself and your most important beliefs—are thought to form the core of your personality and are the best indicators of who you are as a person. If you know yourself well, determining your priorities is relatively easy. However, there are not that many individuals in society who have achieved a high level of personal insight. Most of us continue to struggle within ourselves, looking for experiences that might fulfill and enrich our lives.

> The more information you have about yourself and skiing, the better chance you have of choosing important skiing outcomes.

Figure 2.1
Relationships Between Motivation and Outcome Importance,
Performance Goal Certainty, and Effort Certainty

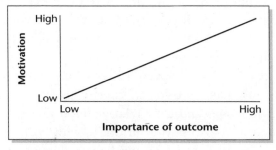

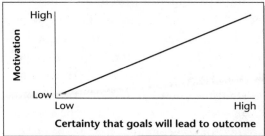

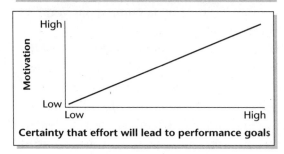

Figure 2.2 describes some of the outcomes that might appeal to your understanding of yourself and your beliefs. These are only suggestions; you should make your own list and prioritize the outcomes by their importance. If you are a beginner, view your list of outcomes and their relative rankings as tentative and subject to change once you begin to ski. If you are a more advanced skier, you'll already have some solid ideas. Just make sure you are constructively critical of your outcomes and their relative importance. It's a good idea to discuss your priorities with others who know you well and who, preferably, have had experience with skiing. We are all limited by our perceptions of ourselves and our abilities, and by our perceptions of skiing. The more information you have about yourself and skiing, the better chance you have of choosing important outcomes. Remember that when you seek advice you are seeking information, not looking for someone to tell you what to do. You alone should make the decision about your best skiing outcomes.

If you're just beginning to ski and are thinking about competing, it's very beneficial to speak with a coach or teacher about your possible outcomes for skiing. This is especially true if you're blessed with talent and are experiencing success. Talented individuals, new to skiing, often let others control their

Figure 2.2
Some Possible Skiing Outcomes

- Being the best skier you can possibly be
- Overcoming challenging environments
- Enjoying beauty and grace
- Identifying with the mountains
- Competing against others
- Expressing yourself
- Experiencing excitement and danger
- Analyzing the technology and science of skiing
- Being with fit people
- Being part of the skiing scene
- Loving the outdoors
- Striving for health and fitness
- Being a World Cup competitor

decision making. This is unhealthy and should be avoided. Remember that winning races or just skiing down the mountain faster than another is only an indication of how you skied at a certain point in time (a performance indication) and not an outcome. Let's take a closer look at a few outcome examples from Figure 2.2.

Being the Best Skier You Can Possibly Be

Becoming a better skier and achieving goals provides feedback that you're improving your skiing abilities.

This is a long-term outcome that can take a lifetime to achieve, because you can always become a better skier. This outcome is attractive for those who value personal improvement and who would become bored if they reached a given level and saw no reason to work at becoming better. This is also an attractive outcome for competitive skiers. You can always find ways to improve and gain more control over your chances for success.

Identifying with the Mountains

Choosing this outcome is an expression of your ability to respond to the challenges put to you by the mountain. This means that you're able to ski and appreciate the beauty and difficulty of skiing while at the same time achieving success in your efforts. This outcome is attractive for those who love being on mountains, who gain strength and security from the mountain environment, and who have a great appreciation for the beauty of mountains. It is also an outcome that skiers at any skill level can achieve. It is interesting to note that this outcome involves personal fitness and skiing skill development as two of its performance goals because it is hard to appreciate any environment when you're exhausted or falling constantly. Once you've achieved a satisfactory level of skill, however, all that's necessary to fulfill this outcome is to be on the mountain skiing.

Experiencing Excitement and Danger

This outcome is attractive for people who want to compete with the mountain and for those who thrive in situations that produce nervous energy. For you to succeed, you must have performance goals that lead to expert skiing. If this outcome appeals to you, be advised that it also means you may continually need to look for new challenges, including the possibility of extreme skiing. Even though the danger may only be in the eyes of those who are watching, to satisfy this outcome you will continually need to determine exactly what is required to succeed, because the alternative to success is very unpleasant. If this outcome is a priority for you, careful planning is critical.

Being a World Cup Competitor

This outcome may be attractive for skiers who are starting to compete or who are actively competing in junior ski competitions. Because of the intensity of the competition, this is a very difficult outcome to achieve. The more time you spend planning, the greater your chances for success; you must carefully consult with coaches and your parents. If this outcome is part of your dream, you can work to make it happen. You are in control of your behavior. Of course you need to be realistic, but don't give up your dream or your plan until the evidence for doing so is overwhelming.

Sometimes coaches and parents aspire to this outcome, but the skier does not share the dream. Because many coaches are former world competitors, they assume that the talented skiers they work with want to become World Cup competitors, too. These coaches, with their assumptions and ambitious goals, can set themselves, their skiers, and their skiers' parents up for frustration. If you are in this situation, you need to have an open, direct discussion with the coach and your parents.

There is certainly nothing wrong with skiing for the love of competition or simply to become the best that you can be. The important thing is not to shut your coaches or your parents out of what you're thinking. Most parents want to help their children accomplish their goals, even if those goals are different from their own.

Competing Against Others

Competition is available to many more skiers now that most mountain ski resorts have set up race departments that not only coach junior skiers but also offer races and clinics for the public and for ski clubs. Expert coaching is available on most mountains in North America. Check with a local ski club or your favorite ski resort. Competitive skiing is an important option for intermediate to advanced skiers who love to compete.

Establishing Performance Goals and Effort Levels

Complementary to and integrated with your core personality are personal characteristics that also influence how you think, behave, and make decisions. Pay attention to these characteristics when you are establishing performance goals, which are the measurable stepping stones to realizing your long-term outcomes.

At the end of the last chapter, you were asked to identify the attention skill with which you are most confident and the three personal characteristics that describe you best. Review those top three personal characteristics now. Search your experiences to support or not support your initial assessment. Talk with others who know you best; if you receive supporting evidence from your investigation, you're probably on the right track. You'll gradually begin to improve your self-knowledge, thus improving your ability to make effective decisions about your outcomes and goals.

> Performance goals are measurable stepping stones to realizing your long-term skiing outcomes.

The Superperson and Variations

The following list shows one of the most common groupings of personal characteristics found in athletics, and I suspect in skiing.

- High confidence in attention skills
- High energy
- High need for control
- High self-esteem
- High competitiveness

This collection of characteristics defines the super-person, to whom you were introduced in Chapter One. Superpersons go through life with zest and confidence. Skiing is an excellent activity for expression of super-person characteristics. Each day of skiing provides challenge, excitement, and new experiences.

If you're a beginning skier with these characteristics, however, it's possible to become frustrated quickly. Skiing is a complex sport that requires learning several new skills. If you have a background in ice skating, rollerblading, or surfing, you may already possess some of the same knowledge and skills required in skiing. If so, you can expect to progress according to your expectations. If you don't have a background in these sports, however, your progression may be a little slower than you expect for yourself, which may lead to your becoming frustrated. Why? Superpersons generally set high standards for themselves and expect success immediately. If this description fits you, it's important for you to obtain qualified instruction and to really listen to your instructors. You will progress much faster under the guidance of a competent and caring instructor than you will gutting it out on your own. If you forgo qualified instruction early in your skiing career, be prepared to take a lot longer to succeed, and to experience quite a bit of frustration along the way.

If you are essentially a superperson and also sensitive, it's even more important to be successful, because you tend to personalize your success or lack of it. If you are this kind of superperson, you must be very objective when you set your performance goals; you thus increase your opportunities for feelings of success and achievement. In effect, you need to reduce what you might think of as your normal expectations of progress, as they may not be realistic. This is especially true if you're a beginner. Check out your performance expectations with a ski coach or instructor or a friend who skis.

If you combine a generally confident outlook with a tendency to evaluate and worry over things rather than make quick decisions, and if you also tend to be critical, you need to be especially careful to set effective performance goals. Pondering or worrying over what you're not doing or not accomplishing can significantly interfere with your capacity to perform and, because you expect to excel, can increase your anxiety. This combination of characteristics can make learning to ski, competing, or just enjoying skiing with friends extremely difficult and frustrating. But don't be alarmed—you

47

don't need to burn your skis! By carefully working out your performance goals, you will know when you're going to improve and learn specific skills, and you will worry less.

Another variation on the superperson model is the generally confident individual who prefers to depend on others for direction. If this characterization describes you, you feel safe as long as you have a significant other—a coach, parent, spouse, or friend—helping you plan. I encourage you to become more involved in your own skiing plan. You need to set your own performance goals. This is especially true for married couples in which each member possesses different capacities and skills. Each person should have his or her own agenda. Once both of you have established and accepted this idea, you will experience fewer conflicts and hurt feelings. Respecting and encouraging each other in your pursuit of individual goals will help to make each ski outing enjoyable.

Young skiers commonly depend on a parent or coach for advice. This advice is great; just remember that the skier should be in charge of his or her own performance goals. If you're a young skier, be sure to use your coaches and parents to *help* you set and achieve your goals. If you're a parent, remember that goals are more meaningful if your child is the one who decides which ones to pursue.

The List Person–Worrier and Variations

The following is another common pattern of personality characteristics:

- Critical
- Prone to worrying
- Sensitive
- Confident in handling analytical problems

This type of person is best described as a list person–worrier. If this description fits you, be sure your plan includes a means for you to obtain constant success feedback. Being critical is a strength, because you tend to be detail oriented, which increases the probability that your goal-setting plan will be effective. By being critical you'll also have a capacity to determine errors and their source more quickly than others do. The way to keep your skiing on a positive and enjoyable keel is to set small performance goals and receive success feedback often. Remember, it isn't how quickly you improve, it's where you arrive in the end. The constant flow of success feedback will help you stay motivated and energized. In addition, keep records of everything. If you're a competitive skier, keep a journal. Viewing your accomplishments will greatly enhance your enjoyment of and motivation for skiing. It will make it easier for you to stick to a long-term plan.

The Free Spirit

We see another somewhat common pattern in the individual who

- Has a lot of energy
- Has the willingness to engage risk
- Lives by personal standards
- Is very positive
- Is not controlled by schedules
- Can become easily distracted from tasks

Although there is no agreed-upon label for this type of person, I sometimes refer to individuals with this constellation of characteristics as free spirits. If this description fits you, you may find yourself going over the same runs, repeating the same errors, and not making improvements in your skiing. This is usually due to an unwillingness to take the time to evaluate your skiing carefully. The best way to alter this pattern is to get regular evaluations from professional coaches or instructors. Their critiques will provide you with information you may have been aware of but not really paying attention to. For you, achieving your performance goals and setting effort levels (which we discuss a bit later in the chapter) is a constant dynamic. For the most

> Remember, it isn't how quickly you improve, it's where you arrive in the end.

effective progression, keep getting outside expert evaluation to help you modify your performance goals and the effort required to achieve those goals.

Goal-Setting Guidelines

We ensure that we stay motivated by determining effective outcomes, performance goals, and effort levels. The following guidelines on how to set effective goals are derived from research conducted over the last thirty-five years in sport and physical activity settings. There is considerable agreement among psychologists regarding the effectiveness of the principles described here. For a more detailed analysis of goal setting, refer to the books by Cox (1994) and Weinberg and Gould (1995) listed in Appendix B.

1. An outcome is what you want to achieve over the long term and represents your most important reason for participating. To be an effective motivator, the outcome should be reachable if you stretch all limits.

2. Your performance goals should also have a realistic chance for success. These goals are specific levels that must be achieved in order to reach your outcome. In setting performance goals, it is important to remember that difficult goals are more motivating than easy goals.

3. You, the skier—not coaches, instructors, or friends—must subjectively determine your realistic chances for success, although these significant others can certainly influence your appraisal of your potential for success.

4. You need to sequence your goals in such a way that you can see the logical progression from effort to goal achievement to outcome achievement. You need to know exactly what performance goals are required to achieve your outcome. You then have to determine how much time it's going to take to achieve your performance goals. The amount of time it takes relates to the effort required to learn and achieve your performance goals.

5. Goals should be measurable, enabling you to easily determine whether or not you've reached your goal.

6. Goals that you set with someone else are usually more difficult to attain than those you set by yourself. If you are discussing your skiing goals with a friend, coach, or teammate, your goals generally will be set higher. (If you're a competitive skier, it's important to involve your coach and family with all of your goals, as these people will be instrumental in helping you aim high.)

7. Performance goals and effort levels are more meaningful if they are under your control. Stay away from goals (for example, skiing faster than another skier in a race) that hinge on the performance of others over whom you have no control. Remember, you have no control over how fast anyone else will ski.

Steps to Motivated Skiing

We've looked at the relationship between understanding one's core personality and selecting appropriate skiing outcomes. We also understand how performance goals need to be established as intermediate stepping stones toward our fulfillment of longer-term outcomes. Using this information, let's look at the actual steps you should take to establish your own goal-setting plan.

Establish Major Outcomes

You need to give this a lot of thought, because, as we have discussed, the more importance you place on the outcome, the more motivated you'll be. We have also noted that the importance of an outcome is determined by how closely the outcome relates to the center or core of your personality. The better you understand yourself, the more likely you are to choose a significant, motivating outcome.

Take some time to think about your possible outcomes and to rank them. Refer once again to the selected outcomes in Figure 2.2, and develop others to match your personality core and your aspirations in skiing. Create at least one personal skiing outcome and write it down. If you have one or two other important outcomes, list them in their order of importance to you.

Personal Skiing Outcomes

1. _____
2. _____
3. _____

Set Performance Goals You Need to Reach in Order to Achieve Your Outcome

Performance goals normally cover a variety of areas: fitness, physical skills, mental skills, skiing knowledge, and knowledge of competition, snow conditions, weather, and equipment. Unless you possess specialized knowledge, you will need to receive expert guidance.

Fitness

Most skiers need to set fitness goals. In getting advice on this performance goal, it's smart to look to professionals in the fitness industry who also know skiing. Your consultant should possess a degree in exercise or sport science from a reputable university, certification from a reputable health fitness organization, or both. He or she should also have knowledge of skiing, because fitness programs and their results are highly specific.

Considering that fitness has not been a major priority with the general adult public in North America, many skiers will need to become more competent in this arena. The older you get, the more important fitness becomes; you start to lose muscle mass at around thirty-five years of age, even if you're still active. Weight training and cardiovascular training can effectively reduce age-related losses of strength and endurance. Smart skiers also know that improved fitness prevents injuries and gives them a margin of safety that less fit skiers don't enjoy.

One of the more enjoyable ways to improve fitness and simultaneously train for skiing is to engage in other sports that complement skiing. The sports that transfer most readily to skiing are rollerblading, ice skating, ice hockey, and possibly mountain biking. These sports not only improve physical fitness for skiing but also involve mental and physical skills that can transfer. Even sports like tennis provide the opportunity for you to practice mental skills.

Physical Skills

You also need specialized knowledge to establish effective goals for developing skiing skills. Skiing is both cognitive and physical. You have to know what skills

55

you need to learn, how you can learn them, and in what order. Once you have this information it's possible to effectively plan your instruction and practice on the mountain. Your consultant in this arena should be expert in learning and in skiing knowledge. In addition to providing a critique of your skiing performance, ski instructors can develop drills for you to work on outside of skiing class.

Mental Skills

Mental skills are essential for skiers. Chapters Five and Six address the basic mental skills you need to develop. For mental skills to be useful when you need them, you must learn and practice them just as you do the physical techniques of skiing.

Skiing Knowledge

Developing knowledge in skiing can be a rewarding experience. There are countless books exploring the many dimensions of skiing. For example, if you're going to be engaging in backcountry skiing, you need to acquire a considerable knowledge base to do it safely; you'll need to become expert on avalanche risks, weather forecasting, snow conditions, and survival skills. Competition is also an area with a large knowledge base; every major university in North America has considerable resources available concerning this subject. Appendix B lists several resources.

Most ski resorts have learning channels that provide the latest instruction techniques for various aspects of skiing. Remember that it is important not only to practice the suggested techniques but to listen to the reasons underlying the techniques. You gain a great deal of confidence when you understand the cognitive basis of the physical skills you're practicing. Smart skiers are knowledgeable skiers.

Let us look now at an example of how performance goals relate to outcomes. A typical intermediate skier (whom we'll call Annie) has selected "being a competent skier" as her number-one outcome. Follow along as she develops a list of appropriate performance goals in support of her outcome.

An important performance goal in becoming a competent skier is to be able to ski double diamond runs with skill. Annie's biggest obstacle to achieving this goal right now is her lack of proficiency at skiing moguls. Because Annie understands the importance of skiing moguls, she's highly motivated to improve her mogul skiing performance as a short-term performance goal.

Outcome 1: To Be a Competent Skier

I. *Performance goal A: Skiing double diamond runs with confidence*

A. *Skiing moguls*

B. [Another short-term performance goal]

C. [Another short-term performance goal]

D. [Still another short-term performance goal]

She then breaks each performance goal down into its component elements:

A. Skiing moguls

1. Making quick turns

2. Adjusting to terrain changes

3. Mental skills

4. Fitness (We'll assume for purposes of our example that Annie is highly fit for the task.)

She further breaks each component element into basic skills or knowledge:

1. Carving turns

a. Balance

   i. Ski on green groomed runs until complete balance is achieved throughout the run.

   ii. Ski blue groomed runs until complete balance is achieved.

   iii. Ski small moguls on blue runs until balance is achieved.

   iv. Ski small moguls on black runs until
       balance is achieved.

    v. Ski large moguls on black runs until
       balance is achieved.

 b. Control: Repeat the balance regimen for
    control, with the emphasis on keeping
    edges in contact with the snow. The focus
    is to be under constant control. As long
    as edges are in contact with the snow, you
    have control.

 c. Rhythm

    i. The same regimen can be used to focus
       on rhythm.

   ii. Take time to think only of the feel of
       what you are doing; add this component
       to all of the previous experiences. Your
       rhythm is unique.

As you can see from this example, the general approach in setting performance goals is first to research the subject, then look at the performance goals you need to achieve to begin moving toward your outcome. The next step is to break each performance goal down into simpler components. For example, learning how to ski moguls may require you to go back to basic turning skills to make sure you possess the correct knowledge and performance skill. Analyzing making turns may cause you to examine mechanical technique to ensure you are executing turns correctly. Continue breaking components into more basic units until you find where you need to start. Where your skill and knowledge put you *now* is your departure point, the place from which you can begin your journey toward attaining your goal.

In Appendix A you'll find a chart for recording your outcomes and their associated performance goals. Feel free to photocopy this chart as necessary. Begin with your number-one outcome and develop a list of measurable, challenging performance goals that will help you achieve it.

Assess the Likelihood of Achieving Your Outcome If You Are Successful in Reaching Each Performance Goal

The closer this likelihood is to 100 percent, the higher your motivation. In our example, Annie set skiing double diamond runs as the main performance goal, and skiing moguls as the short-term performance goal. Annie knows that her inability to ski moguls is her greatest barrier to competence on double diamond runs. She knows that once she masters moguls she will be very close to attaining her main performance goal, and thus her number-one outcome. Because Annie expects that the likelihood of achieving her overall outcome of competence is nearly 100 percent, she is exceedingly motivated to work toward mastering moguls. Mogul mastery is the key to her future success on double diamond runs and to her eventual achievement of her number-one skiing outcome: to be a competent skier.

Establish the Time and Effort Needed to Achieve Your Performance Goals

This step requires you to determine how many hours of instruction and practice you'll need to achieve each performance goal. This is a best estimate of how much time you'll need to spend practicing each skill when you ski. This planning will also provide an estimate of when you'll achieve your performance goal. Your success in skill development is a powerful motivator.

Let's look at Annie's time and effort plan for gaining balance and control in mogul skiing. (Remember that this is just an example to give you ideas for your own planning.)

Skill Development Plan for Balance and Control When Skiing Moguls

Day 1   One-hour semiprivate lesson on turning skills.

One hour skiing green groomed runs working on balance, rhythm, and control.

Evaluate progress.

Day 2   Thirty minutes skiing blue groomed
               runs working on balance, rhythm,
               and control.

               One hour skiing black groomed runs
               working on balance, rhythm, and
               control.

               Evaluate progress and make adjustment
               in plan if necessary.

Day 3   One hour skiing blue groomed runs
               working on balance, rhythm, and
               control for making quick turns.

               One hour skiing moguls on blue run.

               Evaluate progress and make adjustment
               in plan if necessary.

Day 4   One hour skiing moguls on green run.

               One hour skiing moguls on black run.

               Evaluate progress and make adjustment
               in plan if necessary.

Day 5   One hour skiing moguls on black run,
               looking for increasingly difficult moguls.

               Repeat one-hour sessions until confident
               with skill (integrate new mental skills
               with taking air).

               Evaluate progress and make adjustment
               in plan if necessary.

Day 6	One hour skiing moguls on black run. If skill and confidence have been achieved, proceed to double diamond runs. If not, continue practice and evaluation of performance skills.
	One hour skiing double diamond black runs.

In this last one-hour session, Annie has the motor skills necessary to achieve success. Because these runs are steeper and ungroomed with possible large moguls, Annie's main problem will be to integrate the mental skills she has been practicing, specifically to maintain her focus of attention on the task-relevant cues instead of the difficulty of the run.

Day 6 *(continued)*	Evaluate progress and determine what skills and knowledge are needed to continue to build skill and confidence.
Day 7	One hour on black runs practicing the skills that needed work from the previous day.
	One hour on double diamond runs.

On this day Annie finally has a breakthrough and experiences the run she has been waiting for. On the next run, some of the old difficulties return, but she now knows how to handle these difficulties and looks forward to her next ski outing.

Annie would need to work out a similar plan for fitness, mental skills, and learning how to take air. The plan we have just reviewed clearly illustrates how systematic planning can lead to achieving your performance goal, which in turn moves you toward achieving your outcome.

Rate the Likelihood of Achieving Your Performance Goal If You Put in the Time and Effort

The closer your rating is to 100 percent, the greater your motivation. Annie is highly motivated to work on her mogul skiing. She's convinced that once she can handle moguls, she will be able to ski double diamond runs. In this particular case, she rates her chances of achieving the double diamond performance goal at nearly 100 percent.

Evaluate and Adjust as Required as You Progress Through Your Plan

Skiing is a very dynamic sport, so you'll have to make adjustments if busyness or injury impedes your progress. It's also possible that you'll progress faster or slower than you estimated. Small adjustments are the most effective. The important thing is to keep written records of your achievements and progress. Remember that when goals are clear and easy to determine, it's easier to chart your progress. Evaluating your progress, noting it in writing, and making necessary adjustments to your strategic plan can serve as exceptionally strong motivators.

Being organized in the way you set your skiing goals will increase your enjoyment and satisfaction. The Burnett (1994) reference listed in Appendix B is a detailed goal-setting manual that covers every aspect of goal setting for skiing and provides organization charts and journals for record keeping. Although Burnett's book is oriented to competitive ski racers, any skier can use it. In addition to sophisticated manuals like Burnett's, you can use the goal-setting chart in Appendix A to help you get started with determining your outcomes and their associated performance goals.

Once you understand and establish your skiing priorities, you can turn your attention to understanding those variables that influence how fast and effectively you learn. Setting goals is motivating, but understanding learning principles is empowering. In the next chapter we'll look at how to get the most from both your formal instruction periods and your free skiing experiences.

3

Learning to Be
a Smart Skier

After skiing almost all of his first ski season with three of his friends, Tom decided to invest in his first private lesson with a certified instructor. Within a few minutes, the instructor identified the single most important correction Tom needed to make to most efficiently improve his skiing.

Tom acted on the correction a couple of times, and then asked for feedback on other aspects of his technique. The instructor said that she preferred not to comment on anything else until he mastered the first correction. Tom continued practicing, but soon became agitated. "Why aren't you telling me more to do?" he finally complained. She smiled and repeated that she would only make one error correction at a time. "But my buddies used to give me lots of corrections every time I asked for them," he

67

said. "I'd think that, being an instructor, you would be able to find even more things for me to fix."

The instructor smiled again and said, "Detecting errors is only part of helping learners get better at skiing. Another important part is knowing which one error to correct first. That's why we're only correcting your most important error right now. You see, when we are learning, we can really concentrate on only one thing at a time."

Tom looked back with a blank stare as he pondered what she'd said. He nodded and began to smile when the grinning instructor added, "After your skiing buddies become certified instructors, that's probably the first thing they'll learn!"

Imagine that you're riding up the chair lift, and you see three expert skiers flying down the mountain. They look so free and loose that you're amazed. You think to yourself: What would I give to be able to ski like that! How can I become that good? Thinking these thoughts, no matter how skilled you are, you're expressing a desire to learn and excel at this sport. Now you have a choice: you can continue to think and wish, or you can act. By developing a general understanding of the learning process and combining it with an understanding of how you personally learn new skills, you can make great things happen.

This chapter will give you the tools to make ski learning systematic and efficient. It's designed to help you develop a thorough knowledge of skiing, learn new information and skills quickly, and gradually develop the ability to solve your own skiing problems. The first section deals with systematic learning and outlines the skiing knowledge base. A fairly detailed outline of skiing knowledge organization will allow you to tap into your personal knowledge base and build systematically from there. The second section explains how you can efficiently learn new skills and information by applying basic learning principles. The last section provides examples of how you can start analyzing your own ski-related errors and begin problem solving on your own.

When applying learning theory to skiing, it's easy to reduce it to a diagram of little boxes that makes the sport look like a purely mechanical experience. Nothing could be further from the truth. Skiing is a wonderful, even magical experience. I often think that being on a mountain, whether I am skiing or not, is a privilege.

That said, there are advantages now and then to analyzing the sport in a "mechanical" way, particularly when we are discussing what we need to know to master skiing. Because most skiers find that successful performance adds significantly to their skiing experience, and because skiing is expensive, it's really nice to use the time you have on the mountain effectively. Breaking the sport down into its component parts can help you do that. So join me as we delve into the detailed components of learning in general, and ski learning in particular.

Learning About Learning

Your mind is your body and your body is your mind. Nowhere is the unified nature of mind and body more evident than in learning how to ski. Because you're unique, how you learn to ski is going to be unique. Understanding yourself is critical for learning, as it is in knowing what motivates you. Personal characteristics influence how you focus your attention and how you respond to instruction and to newly acquired information and skills. It's also important to remember that you have a unique body structure and system of coordination.

Learning and motivation are intimately related. As you may have noticed in Chapter Two, most goals in skiing require that you learn new information. Learning is what allows you to achieve success and feel competent. Before we look at how personal characteristics influence learning and performance, it's helpful to get a little background on how learning affects our bodies—how we learn and develop coordinated skills. Following that discussion, we'll explore how to use your unique personality to learn quickly and efficiently.

Every time you learn a new skill, your nerve cells connect in a way that allows the idea or representation of the skill to be stored in your brain. As you become better at the skill, coordinated muscular systems develop that allow you to carry out the idea in your head with greater ease and less conscious attention. You travel a three-phase learning path to achieve this advanced level of smooth, almost effortless performance.

Phase One: Creating a Mental Image

The first step in developing coordinated muscular activity is to get a clear image of what we want to perform. Once an accurate image is in our heads, we can make attempts to duplicate it. The image serves as a reference against which we can judge how well we performed. In this first phase of learning, our attempts are often awkward and involve great concentration. As we begin to master the skill, parts of the actual movement sequence become automated. By *automated* here I mean that we don't have to concentrate to perform the skill. We can gradually take our concentration away from the position of our skis, our knee positions, and so on, to concentrate on other aspects of skiing—such as looking where we're going!

If an internal image is important, how do you know you have the correct one? This is an interesting point. One of the coaches at Mammoth Mountain, in the eastern Sierras of California, was a former international competitor from Switzerland. Working with kids under ten years of age, he knew that youngsters are usually very good at duplicating actions. He would often have his students simply follow him down the hill. It was amazing to see all those kids as they mimicked his every move. They all looked like Swiss skiers (which made *them* pretty good models to follow, too).

> The first step in developing coordinated muscle activity is to get a clear image of what we want to perform.

This example points out the benefit of starting to learn how to ski with qualified instructors (for example, those certified by the Professional Ski Instructors Association). It's also a good idea to ask around a little about their backgrounds. If they've been top-level performers, they may be wonderful models to copy. Be aware, though, that an instructor's outstanding skiing expertise does not necessarily correlate with how well he or she communicates. I'm talking here about both the ability of the instructor to explain things and the instructor's warmth, empathy, and other interpersonal characteristics that make learning enjoyable. In addition, to avoid a lot of frustration, you need to be honest about your skills when you sign up for a lesson. It doesn't hurt to tell the ski school what kind of a person you are so that they can match you up with an appropriate instructor. Even better would be to speak with the instructor before your lesson and ask her what she is going to try to achieve. If improved performance is her first objective, be careful: to learn effectively, safety and skill technique are more important.

Beware of copying just any skier you see on the mountain. Over the years it's become fashionable to ski with your boots rubbing together, snaking your way down the mountain. If you watch the best skiers in the world, however, they don't ski this way. You'll see them skiing with their skis almost shoulder-width apart. This posture allows the skier to instantly apply pressure to the skis' edges to keep control. It's your choice, of course. Just decide whether you want to look like a snake or to ski effectively. (You can guess which approach I like best!) Watching videos of the best skiers in the world can help you solidify great mental images.

Phase Two: Developing Associations

As you enter the second phase of learning, you begin to associate signals from inside your body and from the environment with actions, and to associate the actions with consequences. As the positive results of your body's responses increase in frequency, the internal and external signals begin to trigger actions automatically. The more automated the movement becomes, the more you're able to adjust to new and unique situations.

The systematic way to automate each phase of a new skiing skill is to ensure that you understand the appropriate movement sequence. For example, in making a turn you must first have your skis going downhill. Next, you plant your pole to signal the weight shift to the downhill foot, which directs your line of force directly through the inside edge of your downhill ski and the outside edge of your uphill ski. Finally, keeping your legs well flexed and your upper body perpendicular to the ski line as you finish your turn will start the process all over again as your weight is shifted to the downhill foot.

> The more automated the movement becomes, the more you're able to adjust to new and unique situations.

Having separated each part of the sequence, focus your attention on the first part until it's automated, then go to the next part. Once each part of the turn is automated, you must pay attention to the rhythm of skiing. You can learn this rhythm by thinking about nothing but the *feel* of skiing. This proprioceptive feedback is an important component in skiing. Once you recognize the rhythm, it too will become an automated part of your skills, freeing up your attention for learning something else.

Phase Three: Applying and Expanding Cognitive Knowledge

This phase is often called the automated phase of learning, when little or no attention is needed for you to perform specific physical actions. During this phase, you can direct your attention to things other than the act of skiing, applying your cognitive knowledge to solving skiing problems on the mountain. For example, if you have never skied on powder snow but have achieved automated skiing performance on groomed runs, you will need to make an adjustment (this is typical of many skiing problems). You have to make turns—a previously learned skill—but the snow conditions are different. By developing a cognitive understanding of the principles that control your turns, you can apply this knowledge to skiing in powder. Once you have had the opportunity to apply the knowledge to actual skiing in powder, your body will make the needed adjustments in rhythm, control, and balance. Soon you will be making turns in powder as easily as on a packed run. You will have automated skiing in powder, integrating cognitive information with motor skills to solve a skiing problem.

The main point is that you never stop learning, even though you have automated a skill. Each tiny bit of information you pick up can be integrated with prior knowledge to help you solve new problems you encounter. Thus the third phase of learning is a dynamic interaction of acquired knowledge and new experiences and challenges.

As an example of cognitive information that directly influences your skiing performance, take the mental skills and knowledge of skiing techniques (mechanics) needed to understand the relationship between attention to task-relevant cues, limited attention capacity, and skiing performance. Our fantastic learning system works very well most of the time. Unfortunately, because we also have the ability to think, we can interfere with the system and either cause delays or wreck our coordination outright. For example, if you can negotiate a turn effectively on fairly level terrain, why is it that the turn doesn't flow as easily when you get on a steep slope? The most likely reason is that on a steeper pitch you become distracted with thoughts of the fall you might take. You then attempt to protect yourself from such a fall by leaning into the mountain, which ruins your ability to turn. The result, of course, is an uphill fall—something you could have avoided by using your understanding of the importance of task-relevant cues and limited attention capacity and your ability to focus on those cues.

Learning more about the technical aspects of skiing in powder can help you learn. For example, the application of force through your skis is slightly different in powder than on a packed run, because your skis are almost or completely covered with snow, causing altered resistance. Putting your weight slightly back on your heels causes the tips of your skis to rise. This adjustment allows you to regain control of your downhill course and to make effective turns. The rhythm needed will be noted and learned. The basic principles of your turn carving are the same, but you have been able to adjust to different snow conditions—another example of the dynamic flexibility and effectiveness of your learning and performance system.

Thanks to their wealth of experience, the best skiers in the world have an incredible number of automated programs at their disposal. Think of Franz Klammer's great Olympic gold medal performance in which he lost his balance near the end of the run. He was traveling at over eighty miles per hour at the time, yet he regained his balance. How did he do this? His balance skill was highly learned and automated. As soon as his body recognized the imbalance, Klammer instantly began to correct the movement without any conscious thought whatsoever. In effect, one of his balance programs took over without his having to consciously direct it to do so. If he had said to himself, "Gee, I am falling. I must make a correction," he would probably not be alive today. It takes about a quarter of a second for us to recognize a thought and initiate a movement.

At eighty miles per hour, Klammer would have traveled a minimum of twenty-nine feet during the time needed to begin making a correction if he had had to think about it. By the time he initiated his correction, he would have been far off the course and unable to avoid one of the downhill barricades or a natural obstacle on the mountain. You saw what happened to Hermann Maier in the 1998 Olympic downhill.

For highly patterned skills, humans have the capacity to adjust instantly to the demands of the situation. The lesson here is that the more skill you can build into your body, the better you'll be able to adjust to the demands facing you. This is not instinctual, but a response based on learning. The only instinctual part is the genetic potential your parents gave you. Once you learn a skill, it's in your body for as long as your nervous system works. The importance of mental techniques, which we'll cover in later chapters, is that they give you the freedom to avoid such distractions as overanalysis, fear, and self-criticism. This freedom allows you to automate your skiing over a variety of environmental conditions.

You need to be able to recall or adjust using previously learned skills if you want to ski with the poise and effectiveness of a champion like Franz Klammer. Here's a personal illustration to emphasize the difference between the performances of elite and intermediate skiers. I was learning how to make turns when I had the opportunity to ski with my friend Kevin Burnett, an Olympic coach who recently retired from the U.S. ski team. He suggested that no matter the speed at which you need to carve a turn, it's still the same skill. At the top of the mountain, he leaped off a ten-foot lip shouting, "This is how it looks in the textbooks, Dennis." The hill

> Once you learn a skill, it's in your body for as long as your nervous system works.

was very steep, and covered with five-foot moguls. Kevin was often as much as ten feet in the air between periodic contacts with the snow. He landed in perfect balance, turned on whatever he landed on, and returned to the air. After he went down the entire run, I was to follow.

You might guess what happened. I was neither in control in the air nor able to negotiate landings and turns at such high speeds. I had to slow frequently to regain control. My skiing was just embarrassing compared to Kevin's.

I needed to learn how to get in better control while taking air and also to learn landings and turns under varied conditions. I have been practicing ever since, and after many days of skiing difficult slopes, I am finally able to make some of the adjustments simply by responding to the mountain without thinking things through. You can develop these abilities only by practicing repeatedly over time with specific goals in mind—in my case, the goals of landing under control and not becoming intimidated by the steepness of the slope.

We have been talking about learning that goes on well beyond the automation of the skill. Increased knowledge and practicing under variable conditions increase the skill complexity that you can call on when you need it. The more varied your practice conditions, even after the basic skill is automated, the more flexible your motor control system becomes. That is what improves your chances of making instant adjustments to the challenges of any run. You increase your knowledge base best by skiing, knowing what you're doing, talking with other skiers and professional instructors, and reading. What you are thinking about or what you are concentrating on is what you are telling your body to do.

> Practicing under variable conditions increases the skill complexity you can call on when you need it.

This point is crucial to remember in your quest to improve as a skier. It underscores how important it is to know yourself and what your long-term goals are, to clarify the performance goals and effort requirements needed to reach those goals, and to act on them. It also reinforces the importance of developing the mental techniques that give you the freedom to practice your physical skills.

Personal Factors and Learning

You have probably noticed in our discussion so far that it's very important to focus your *attention* on specific information in order to learn. Initially, you focus on the image, then on automating each part of the skill, and finally on expanding your understanding of the skill under a variety of environmental conditions. Your ability to attend to information, like other personal factors, is based on your genetics and your experience.

In the first phase, you must focus only on the image; this requires you to narrow your attention and shut out all distractions except the image you're watching. The sooner you can begin attempting to duplicate the image with actual practice, the better off you are. Also, if you or your instructor can apply skills you have learned elsewhere to skiing, you'll automate the skill faster. For example, if you know how to ice skate or rollerblade, you have the necessary knowledge to balance and control your body on skis. You'll need to understand the specific skiing elements, but the skill knowledge is in your body to begin with. This has the effect of reducing the amount of information you'll have to attend to and learn.

Once you've started physical practice, you'll then focus your attention on the feedback that you're getting from your body and probably from an instructor. Your attention is limited to one thing at a time, so attend to making only one correction at a time. If your instructor gives you more than one correction, ask her what is most important and work only on that one. When you have mastered the most important correction, move to the next most important correction.

> What you are thinking about or what you are concentrating on is what you are telling your body to do.

Other personal factors can influence your rate of skiing-related learning. I believe the most critical are confidence, concentration, instructor relations, and control. Let's take a look at each of these.

Confidence

Confidence in your attention skill is highly individual. If you're good at interpreting a lot of things going on in the environment, you'll easily be able to follow the moves of a skilled model. If you combine this with the ability to narrow your focus and shut out distractions, then you'll be better able to duplicate what you see. Many of us have a tendency to want to get moving and not listen to anyone speaking. If you're more analytical or are good at handling a lot of things going on in your head, then you'll be able to watch the model, internalize this model in your head, and go over it repeatedly until you get a chance to practice the skill physically. The more analytical you are, the more acceptable verbal comments are. Once you start physical practice, you'll likely have to remind yourself to let everything happen, or to "get out of your head." When it's time to move, let yourself move; don't try to think while you're moving.

If you do not possess attention skill confidence you will need to work at improving these skills. You can refer to "Attention Control Training" in Chapter Six.

Concentration

Careful laboratory studies have demonstrated that we can only pay attention to one thing at a time. While you're learning skills, all of your concentration is focused on learning. As you acquire more and more motor skills, you will need to pay less and less attention to them. If you're having difficulty carving turns on green runs, you're going to have trouble on steeper runs. This is because you can focus only on limited information. For example, if you must focus attention on various aspects of carving a turn, it will be impossible for you to attend to other aspects of skiing (such as knowing where you're heading).

If you are still focusing on learning specific skills, you are likely to be very surprised by increases in speed, changes in terrain, or obstacles. This limited ability to concentrate explains why beginners commonly crash into other skiers. They are so focused on staying up or negotiating a turn that it's impossible for them to focus on other skiers. Give beginners lots of room. They are trying the best they can currently manage and are helpless to respond to other skiers. We have all seen insensitive skiers shouting at beginners to get out of the way. Such behavior is inappropriate, and the individuals who engage in it are at a low level of evolutionary development. By the same token, it's best for skiers who are just beginning to ski on slopes for beginners until they can use their new skills without having to focus on their actual performance. You'll easily recognize a new stage of advancement when you find yourself moving down a slope and actually looking to see where you're going.

Your ability to concentrate is influenced by anxiety and arousal. Whether or not you get anxious learning to ski is determined by your personality characteristics. It is generally recommended that you stay calm and focused when you are learning. It's OK to be excited, as long as you can concentrate effectively. If you experience stress while learning how to ski, you'll need to develop a relaxation skill to assist your learning process. Relaxation techniques, and explanations of why anxiety occurs in the first place, are described in more detail in Chapters Five and Six.

Instructor Relations

How you relate to your instructor is influenced by your personality. A self-confident person tends to accept constructive criticism well, whereas a more sensitive person may begin to question his or her abilities when given such feedback.

In our culture, instructors generally make an effort to be positive, or to put corrective feedback in positive forms. For example, a positive instructor might say something like, "I like most of your turning technique, but if you bend your knees a little more, your turns will be even better." This approach assumes that by being positive, instructors create a more positive attitude about skiing. If you're a more critical individual than the instructor, he may lose credibility in your eyes, particularly when you perceive that you're making a lot of mistakes. In the face of positive feedback, you may tell yourself that the instructor isn't honest or isn't a very good observer because you know that your turns are just awful. On the other hand, if you're a very positive person and you have a critical instructor—one who might say, for example, "Your knees are completely wrong. Bend them!"—you may have a tendency to blow off many of her comments. As a more positive individual, you may counter the instructor's message by telling yourself that your knees couldn't possibly be completely wrong. In both negative and positive forms, the real message is "Bend your knees."

The key is simply to remember what you and the instructor are trying to do—namely, help you learn how to ski better. Most instructors will give you feedback that can help you do just that. Listen to what the instructor says only as a source of information, then evaluate the usefulness of the information. You can thus avoid personal interference, no matter the source.

Control

If you have a high need for control, you may have a tendency to struggle with anyone giving you instructions. This characteristic will retard your learning if it prevents you from listening effectively to an instructor. Most individuals are willing to give up control in situations that demand it, and learning how to ski is one of those situations.

Systematic Ski Learning

Systematic learning in skiing is similar to building a house. When constructing a new home, it's smart to build your foundation before you build your floors and walls. It's difficult to put windows in a house if you don't have walls. With a good plan, you accomplish one task at a time, and the house eventually takes shape. In the same manner, you can build your knowledge of skiing. It's very difficult to ski a double diamond run if you have not mastered basic skiing skills. If you systematically build your knowledge in the correct sequence, stacking one brick of knowledge on another, becoming an expert skier is fun and enjoyable.

Figure 3.1 outlines the knowledge systems in skiing. Looking at the figure you'll note that all ski knowledge can be divided into five major areas: technology and equipment, training and fitness, mental and motor skills, learning and instruction, and applied knowledge systems. Within each of the major areas there are a number of individual components. These are not listed in order of importance or in chronological order. They are all important, and you should learn them whenever the opportunity for exploring an area presents itself. (Appendix B lists references that provide more detailed information on the subjects we won't cover in this book.) This book emphasizes the major building blocks of mental and motor skills and learning and instruction.

As in any area of study, we can break components down into more detailed components. Figure 3.2 illustrates the breakdown of mental and motor skills. As you can see from the figure, motor skills break down into basic motor skills, advanced motor skills, and specialized motor skills. In turn, each of these has subcomponents worthy of many hours of attention and practice. Likewise the mental skills break down into the components of emotional control, concentration skill, and motivation skill. Chapter Two showed how the subcomponents of self-awareness and goal setting can be expanded to give insights into how we become and remain effectively motivated. In a similar way, Chapters

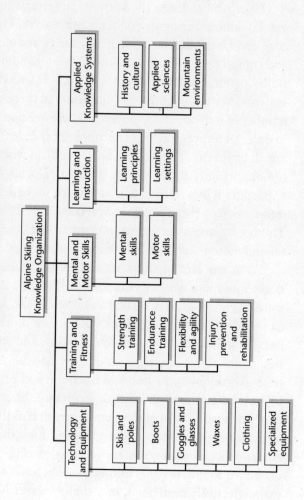

Figure 3.1
Alpine Skiing Knowledge Organization

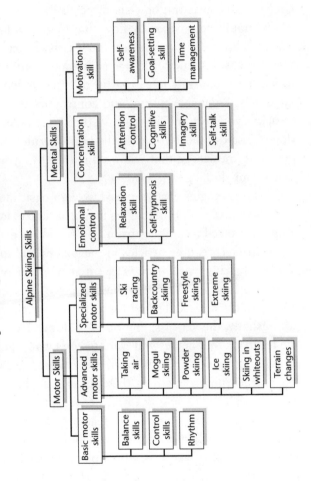

Figure 3.2
Alpine Skiing Motor and Mental Skills

Five and Six expand on the mental skills of emotional control and concentration skill, respectively.

It should be obvious by now that there is a lot to learn to become an expert skier, and it's easy to see why you can easily spend a lifetime skiing and continuing to learn. Of course you can begin to enjoy skiing immediately. Balance, rhythm, and control are the only "bricks" you need initially to have fun skiing on easier slopes. You can then systematically begin learning other pieces of knowledge that will eventually allow you to reach your skiing goals.

Acknowledging that you need to learn basic motor skills first does not mean that it's inappropriate to learn about advanced techniques from books and ski magazines. In fact, reading articles in magazines and journals or talking with friends is often what inspires people to look into skiing in the first place. However, you learn the basic skills first for a very important reason: usually, the act of skiing down a slope gives you the feedback that makes you want to come back. Some individuals want to return to the ski hill for the challenge of learning something they perceive as difficult. Some are attracted simply to the sensual feedback of sliding down snow on skis. Because the act of skiing itself is powerfully motivating, your motor skill learning should take place as soon as possible. Cognitive information (such as applied scientific principles of training, learning, and execution), which is indeed crucial in helping you become an expert skier safely and enjoyably, is most helpful when you introduce it after you've begun to develop your motor skill abilities. The bottom line: get out on the snow as soon and as often as you can.

Humans have the capacity to solve problems. It's what distinguishes us from lower animal forms. You need knowledge to solve problems—generally, the more knowledge you have the more problems you can solve. However, developing your knowledge *systematically* is what allows you to solve problems quickly and easily. Developing your skiing knowledge is very similar to learning math or any other subject: the more principles you understand, the easier problem solving becomes.

Close examination of Figures 3.1 and 3.2 will reveal a logical progression to learning. It's essential that you learn the basic skills of control, rhythm, and balance before progressing to the advanced skills. Remember, learning progression is not just performing a turn on the bunny runs but rather gradually progressing from beginning to intermediate runs. Increased challenge will come from steeper terrain and more speed. Once you begin to learn how to carve the turn, your balance and control improve, and you can ski at the speed your fitness and ability allow.

Notice that I've introduced the word *fitness*. As you increase your speed, it takes more strength and muscular endurance to maintain control of your center of gravity through your feet and skis. If you find yourself becoming fatigued quickly, to the point that your thighs feel like they are burning up, either you are using incorrect technique, or the muscular strength and endurance in your legs doesn't support your skiing ability. In the latter case, you need to develop the appropriate knowledge about fitness training and start a training program to complement your skiing. Many skiers who think they are fit find out differently when they challenge their limits on the mountain. This mention of fitness serves also to emphasize the integrated nature of skiing knowledge. Although this book is focused on mental and physical skills, the entire knowledge system becomes increasingly relevant as you approach more challenging ski goals, particularly if you want to get into the more advanced areas—backcountry skiing, ski racing, extreme skiing, and the like.

The integrated nature of skiing knowledge is further illustrated by programs that teach youngsters how to race. Junior ski programs around the country do an excellent job of teaching youngsters how to ski. These kids do amazing things on skis; however, as the level of competition increases, skiing becomes more difficult. For one thing, the increased physical size of growing junior racers results in a tremendous increase in speed. The risks of injury become greater when skiers travel at speeds in excess of fifty miles per hour. Not many programs teach kids how to deal with the fear that these increased speeds is bound to arouse. In addition, these kids are going through all the joyful trials of adolescence. How many programs teach children how to deal with the typical problems of adolescence? Ski coaches possess tremendous skill and are expert in their knowledge of skiing, as most have had very successful ski racing careers. However, that experience does not provide these competent individuals with knowledge about growth and development issues, unless they also happen to be teachers or parents, in which case they have been exposed to these knowledge systems. Integrating information is difficult, yet it's the key to meaningful instruction and learning.

Let us look now at the sequence of events most likely to ensure that learning will be efficient, safe, and enjoyable.

1. *Develop a plan.* We looked at the technique for planning and goal setting in Chapter Two. Your plan should be realistic, dynamic (easily altered), and measurable.

2. *Learn basic motor skills.* Gradually increase the steepness on groomed runs until you're skiing intermediate groomed runs with ease and skill. As you develop your confidence in early learning, avoid moguls.

3. *Learn to take air; learn to relax.* The first part of mogul skiing will require you to transfer your balance, rhythm, and control skills to the bumps. However, to

reach an advanced skill level, you will need to leave the ground temporarily, or take air. It's therefore recommended that you learn how to take air early on in learning how to ski moguls. Taking air is easy to learn and adds a real sense of accomplishment and enjoyment to your skiing. Get instruction in this skill so that your learning is safe and enjoyable.

At this point in your learning you may be having trouble concentrating because you're also dealing with high emotions. If this is the case, begin learning a relaxation technique, which will allow you to regain control of your attention so you can focus on task-relevant cues. Jump ahead to the relaxation information in Chapter Five if you need help with anxiety control at this point. If you're not having this type of problem, just continue with the motor skill knowledge system presented here.

4. *Learn to ski moguls.* This skill will take a lot of practice and can be one of the most difficult challenges in skiing. It can be physically demanding, even for expert skiers, depending on the difficulty of the terrain. The good news is that you can control the difficulty of the moguls you ski. Again, I strongly recommend that you obtain qualified instruction in learning mogul technique.

5. *Learn to ski under variable snow and weather conditions.* This means learning how to ski in powder, wind, cold, and icy conditions. Depending on your geo-

graphical location, you can learn these skills earlier in the sequence. Learning how to ski on icy terrain, in deep powder, and through extremes of wind and cold is essential if you live in an area where these conditions routinely occur.

6. *Learn mental skills.* As mentioned earlier, you may need to begin this sooner in the sequence, depending on your own abilities and the stresses that you perceive. At about this point in the learning process (about the time you consider yourself an intermediate skier), you may have a desire, and the ability, to ski more difficult terrain. The diamond and double diamond runs become a realistic challenge. When you enter this stage, you máy run into the fear factor and begin questioning your sanity. You need to evaluate your skills carefully and determine whether you can ski on expert slopes. It's not a crime to negotiate these slopes slowly the first few times. If you find that you're not using the skills that you've mastered in the earlier steps, you're likely suffering from a mental problem that can be solved by learning the basic mental skills. Refer to Chapters Five and Six for an overview of the following types of mental skills:

- Emotional control skills. These skills are useful if such emotions as fear, frustration, and anger are part of your skiing experience. These emotions will often prevent you from being physically ready and able to concentrate on task-relevant cues.

- Concentration skills. These skills are the ones that determine what you focus your attention on. If you have too many things going on in your mind before you begin your run, you may need to practice narrowing your attention focus. If you're missing cues in the environment or not thinking clearly about how you're going to ski the run, you may need to develop scanning skill. Imagery and self-talk can be important tools in developing these capacities.

7. *Learn to ski difficult terrain.* This stage can be sequenced by gradually increasing the difficulty of the runs you ski. Dramatic increases in difficulty expose you to risk of serious injury. By remaining at each new level of difficulty until you're skiing with confidence and skill, you avoid unnecessary risk. Of course, for the most difficult runs, there may be risk even for expert skiers. You should not attempt these runs unless you clearly understand the risks and possess the mental and physical skills to handle them successfully. I can remember refusing to ski a difficult, high-risk run because I could not control my fear. My skiing skills would have been seriously hindered under such circumstances, so

my choosing to ski a less demanding route was the right thing to do. If you are worrying about anything other than the task-relevant cues needed to ski successfully, you should never begin a run that could result in serious injury.

This last step is probably never mastered. We can always keep looking for more challenges. We can always wonder if we have reached our skiing potential. It is this search and wonder that stimulates some individuals to ski the backcountry and in ever more extreme conditions. (One can also sequence the planning and knowledge that goes into these challenging experiences so as to minimize even the risks in extreme conditions.)

Key Learning Principles in Skiing

The more we can learn about learning, the easier learning becomes. The following learning principles govern our ability to concentrate, use memory, and develop coordinated movement patterns. For skiers, understanding these principles can mean the difference between success or failure in learning to ski systematically and effectively. Look the following four principles over and see if you can find practical applications for your own ski learning program. Figure 3.3 summarizes the principles.

Figure 3.3
Key Learning Principles

- We have a limited attention capacity.
- We vary in our ability to learn from a demonstration or model.
- We recall knowledge from memory cues.
- We approach excellence when we practice under varied conditions.

We Have a Limited Attention Capacity

Our ability to concentrate on learning only one thing at a time has serious implications for learning to ski. In order to systematically acquire a new skill, you must understand its movement sequence. Once you know the sequence, you can then concentrate on learning the first part of the sequence until it's automated. You then move on to the second part of the sequence, then the third, and so on until the sequence is completed. Using this technique, you don't waste time. You take maximum advantage of your instruction and practice experiences. Also, because you know that you're going to learn the skill eventually, you don't waste time and energy worrying about what you can't do. It's the smart way to learn skiing skills. There are plenty of books on skiing skills that you can refer to gain the understanding and breakdown of skiing's most common motor skills. Appendix B lists a few of these references.

We Vary in Our Ability to Learn from a Demonstration or Model

As we already know, each person is unique. One of the most graphic illustrations of this point is the way in which individuals watch and then duplicate a model performance. Some individuals are gifted in their ability to develop coordinated motor patterns from watching another person perform, even from only one demonstration. This ability has both positive and negative aspects. Although it is beneficial in that the lucky skier can obtain immediate success feedback, it can be detrimental if the skier never understands the movement sequence or why it should be done in that particular way. Such skiers may not be able to problem-solve for themselves if they run into mistakes or new adaptations that were not demonstrated. In contrast, consider the individual who takes longer to learn the skill, who has to work at understanding what they are doing, and who therefore develops a cognitive knowledge about the skill. In the long run, these less gifted skiers can become much better skiers.

If performing from a model or demonstration is easy for you, you would be smart also to obtain cognitive knowledge about the skills you're performing. If performing from a model or demonstration is more difficult for you, stick with it. The information you obtain from observing the model and processing the sequences, and from trial and error will help you become an independent problem solver in the future.

We Recall Knowledge from Memory Cues

This is an important principle for skiing. One example that illustrates this concept is remembering to turn your skis down the fall line. This is the precise point in carving a turn when you've just completed your turn and it's time to shift your weight downhill. The cue for the downhill shift in weight for many skiers is the pole plant. Once the pole plant becomes associated with the rhythm of the downhill shift in weight, the action becomes automated without active thinking or attention. The pole plant is the memory cue; it triggers the motor program for making the turn. That kind of skiing is smart skiing.

Racers use the gates to cue their weight shift. Their memory of the gate number or another course location cues their adjustments to terrain changes. You can also use cues for handling bumps. When you go over a bump, you need to have flexible legs. The visual cue of the bump can be the reminder to relax your legs. Of course, we learn many cues without awareness. In general, however, the more conscious we are of these cues, the faster we can learn and associate the correct responses.

We Approach Excellence When We Practice Under Varied Conditions

If you are challenged, and you are too late with the correct response or you fail to respond at all, either you have not learned the skill well enough to ski as fast as you were traveling, or the terrain you were skiing was too difficult. In skiing, things happen very fast. If you're traveling down the mountain quickly, you don't have time to think about what you're going to do. Your motor control system can only perform if you've learned the skill well enough that you don't need to think about it. By the same token, if you're traveling down the fall line and you're not challenged by the run, you probably can take on more severe terrain.

Problem Solving in Skiing

This final section deals with problem solving, or the integration of knowledge systems to solve problems. If you've applied proper goal-setting techniques in building your knowledge of skiing, you'll be aware of what you know and what you don't know. You will have structured your skiing experiences to gradually build your skiing knowledge base.

Earlier in this chapter I likened this gradual buildup of knowledge to the organized way in which a house is constructed. When you've achieved your outcomes for skiing, we can say that you've built your own personal ski house. Just as with a real house, however, after you've built it, there always seem to be changes and improvements that still need to be made. Even before you've achieved your planned outcome, you'll be planning additions or changes. Just remember to always build your knowledge in the proper sequence.

Beginning Skiers

When you are a beginner, it's easier to establish your priorities for learning. As we have already discussed, for the majority of beginning skiers, knowledge begins with learning how to ski down a mountain. The first thing to do is break down the motor skills into sequential steps, starting at the first part of the movement sequence. Once you begin to learn the sequence in order, you're starting to build your ski house. Figure 3.2 illustrates the basic learning sequences for control and stability skills in carving turns, and the subsequent learning sequences.

Intermediate Skiers

If you're an intermediate skier, you'll need to review the basic skills in Figure 3.2 and make sure that you can perform these skills without thinking about them. If you can perform these skills on intermediate runs but not on black diamond runs, you need to analyze your fitness level to make sure that you have the strength and endurance to ski steeper and faster slopes. It's also possible that the reason you're not skiing the steeper slopes is that you have a concentration problem. You need to determine the source of your problem.

Do you need to learn the skills better? This might be the solution if you have not spent much time skiing steeper runs, you have no trouble skiing intermediate runs, and you just don't react fast enough to what is happening. In this case you can plan a series of skiing experiences in which the slope and difficulty of the runs gradually increase. In this way you'll gradually develop the skills to handle turns and terrain changes more quickly.

Do you need to improve your fitness level? The answer to this question is generally yes, because improved fitness for skiing will allow you to ski faster and longer without fatigue. If your legs are tiring to the point of burning up almost immediately after initiating a tough run, or if you begin to fall without warning, your fitness level is probably not high enough to support your need to ski difficult terrain. Skiing while tired is not only frustrating and detrimental to your personal enjoyment, but also dangerous. Skiing is not a risk-free sport: there is always the chance of injuring yourself or others because you can't respond to the demands of the situation. Preparation is the best solution to this problem. Speaking of fitness, I once rode a chair lift with a seventy-five-year-old skier who told me he skied almost every day during the winter. I asked him what he did the rest of the year. He looked up at me with a smile on his face and said, "Train." Proper training not only makes your skiing experience less of an endurance contest but also allows you to enjoy skiing runs that you may not have thought possible.

Your problem with skiing steeper and more difficult runs may not be caused by fitness limitations. If you can effectively ski difficult runs on certain occasions and not others, you may have a concentration problem. A common example is a person who can ski difficult runs only when they are located on the bottom half of the mountain, despite the fact that the steepness and difficulty at the top of the run is the same. These kinds of problems and what to do about them are covered in Chapter Six.

Advanced Skiers and Racers

Many advanced and intermediate skiers are turning to ski racing to increase their enjoyment and appreciation for this sport. Race departments at ski areas across the country are offering instruction, training, and race facilities for individuals and groups. Most larger urban centers in North America have ski clubs that plan regular trips to the mountains. These groups are great avenues for beginning racing and are also excellent ways to enhance the social aspect of skiing. Ski resorts also have information on programs they offer and on groups that use their facilities.

Ski racing offers fun and challenges for more advanced skiers. In keeping with our systematic learning approach, however, remember to analyze the motor and mental skills related to ski racing. Actual competition adds a whole new dimension to skiing for most individuals; one of the most positive side effects is that such competition requires increased cognitive knowledge and demands that you gain greater independence in solving your own ski-related problems.

We've discussed motivation and the personality characteristics that help establish the kind of skier you want to be. We've also looked at how goal setting and learning interact to help you reach your objectives. Personality, motivation, learning, and performance are interwoven in any human endeavor. Personality characteristics influence our motivation. Motivation determines the rate and effectiveness of our learning. In turn, learning has a powerful influence on our performance. And because the "bottom line" goal of this book is to improve your skiing performance (and the enjoyment that comes from it), that is where we now turn our attention.

4

High Performance Skiing

I was going down a ski slope with my Uncle Den. I said I wanted to go to the steepest part of this run where a whole bunch of rocks were. He was very experienced at skiing, because he grew up doing it. So when he said, "Do you think you could ski it?" I said yes because he would be close by. I went down the slope making fast turns. I thought that there was a big jump that I could take and get big air.

I zoomed down and was kinda scared because it was big and I found out about two or three feet away, it was a seven-foot rock cliff. I freaked out and stopped, slid over a little bit, and clung on. My uncle was below me, so it was hard for him to get up. He started climbing up the steep slope with his skis perpendicular to the slope. I was really scared, because it was hard to hang on. A skier came down the mountain and stopped.

He tried to lift me up, but it was too hard for him with his skis on. He asked me if I was OK and I said "no!" Two snowboarders came down to see what was happening. With the three of them and my uncle Den calming me down, I gradually worked my way across the top of the cliff. When my uncle reached me the three others left and we slowly worked our way down the really steep part of the slope. I was so relieved. I popped on my skis and went down the hill. At lunch I had a lot to tell.

I felt this was a great experience for me because it showed that I had to stay calm to get out of a difficult situation like that.

—Ian McLorg, age ten

Performance is what you can do, your response to a situation, at one point in time. It's helpful to think of performance as your ability to carry out whatever you must do.

Your performance may vary quite a bit from day

to day. Even if you are normally excellent at what you do, there is no guarantee that on any particular day you'll be excellent. And although under normal circumstances your performance on a task reflects what you have learned and your ability to carry it out, how well you actually perform—on an examination, for example—may not in fact reflect what you know.

Performance Principles

In Chapter Three we discussed principles of learning that are related to performance; let's review them now.

1. *Your ability to concentrate on more than one thing at a time is extremely limited.* You therefore need to concentrate primarily on what is going to make you successful, or you run the risk of making a mistake. It was impossible for Ian to consider his skiing options when he was focused on fear. Remember that what you are concentrating on is what you are telling your body to do. If you need to negotiate a turn, you must be concentrating on whatever allows you to make that turn.

2. *The more skiing skills you've learned and automated, the more likely you will be able to respond to the challenges of the run.* Mental skills help free you to automate your responses. In Ian's case, because the slope was much steeper than he anticipated, he knew

he did not possess the skills to get down the steepest part. This knowledge also increased his fear.

3. *Your coordinated response is controlled not only by your ability to move efficiently and effectively but by your experiences in developing control, rhythm, and balance.* The more varied the terrain and snow conditions you ski, the more adjustments you learn and the better your response to the mountain. Since Ian had never skied on such a steep slope before, he did not know how to respond, and so he froze. Ian simply could not continue to ski; fear caused his body to completely tense up. Once he was down the steep part, his normal confident behavior returned, and his fear immediately left him.

4. *When you ski down a hill, you're going to do it your way.* Individual differences are a fact of life. For example, consider two individuals in the same music class. They play a specific piece of music that they both know by heart. Their performances will be different because each will have his or her own way of presenting the music. You'll never see two individuals walk with the exact same gait pattern, or hear two individuals read a sentence with the exact same tone and expression. These personal distinctions are part of what make each of us unique. You are unique; there is nobody else exactly the same anywhere in this world.

Why am I making such a big deal about this? Because if you understand this concept, you can appreciate whatever you look like on a given day. Many beginners wistfully look at skilled skiers effortlessly zooming down the mountain. They're wistful because they want to ski like the skilled individuals they observe. Forget it! Even if you were just as skilled at skiing (learning) as an expert skier, the two of you would ski differently nonetheless.

It is great to look at skilled skiers, but only to see what you can learn from them. It can also be beneficial to use the model of an excellent skier as a goal and commit yourself to being able to ski that well in the future. When you ski down the mountain, appreciate your run for what it is; don't compare how you looked with anybody else. Appreciate your own skill and style. If you are motivated and you continue to learn, your performance will improve over time.

Why worry about how others ski? Even in competitive skiing, your performance is judged by how fast *you* ski down the run, not by how fast another skier goes down. If another skier is faster on a given day, it's beyond your capacity to do anything about it. You can influence only your own race time. That is the one thing over which you have control.

Performing Under Pressure

Human performance in athletic competition has been a topic of great interest to athletes and sport psychologists for more than thirty-five years. We have developed some knowledge about performing under pressure—which is what skiing is all about. Skiers are constantly challenged by incredible conditions.

Consider the following example. I was skiing recently at Whistler Mountain in British Columbia, one of the most popular and highly rated ski resorts in North America. I was having fun near the top of the mountain when a cloud system suddenly swept in. Immediately other skiers and I were in a whiteout so severe that we could not see our skis. The slope was powder and very steep. I started to panic, not wanting to move. At the same time, I knew that it was a time for clear thinking, not panic. I was lucky when a local skier, who knew the mountain, appeared beside me, and I was able to follow him out of the cloud. How would I have performed alone under those circumstances? I'll never know, but it makes me appreciate how our usual performance can be significantly affected both by internal thoughts and feelings and by external conditions.

> If you are motivated and you continue to learn, your performance will improve over time.

Every day that you ski, you'll face performance challenges. Why is it that you can ski beautifully when you're by yourself, but when you're trying to impress another person, you often underperform? If you're a competitive skier, why do you have great practice runs but sometimes fail to live up to your abilities during competition? The answers to these questions are found in our understanding of concentration.

Concentration

Concentration is a skill you can learn, just as you learned to speak or to ride a bicycle. It's certainly strange to me that we learn so many things in school, yet something as important as concentration is not part of the usual curriculum. Strange, indeed, in that we need to concentrate simply to survive every day. It's important in school, our jobs, our relationships, and in sport. In skiing it's critical.

Consider for a moment how improper concentration can affect performance. A national team member blew out his knee joint by catching his ski tip on a gate repeatedly. After his first injury and rehabilitation, he was naturally concerned about not reinjuring his knee. This concern caused him to re-create the image of the ski catching the gate. What he was really thinking was that he did not want to injure himself again; however, what the image did was activate the motor control system for catching the gate. Because he was so highly skilled, he was able to catch the gate again in almost exactly the same way as in the original accident. It was only a matter of time until he blew his knee out again. Had he known that thinking about an act can actually cause an athlete to perform the same act, he could have refocused his attention on skiing the run. He may have hurt himself again, but it would not have been caused by his own thinking.

If all you have to do is think about what you want to do and you'll do it, what is the problem? The concept is simple, but actually controlling what you're thinking may not be that easy to do. Under normal circumstances, most of us have no problem concentrating. We get up in the morning and manage to get ourselves to school or to work. It's when we're facing pressure that we have trouble controlling our thoughts. A good example is the first time you ski a run that is steeper and more difficult than anything you've previously skied. Fear can start to take hold of you. Pretty soon you feel your body tensing up, and you feel as though it hurts to move. Instead of being focused on where you're going to ski and how to ski the run, you're thinking about self-preservation. The way you keep from falling down the hill is to lean into the mountain. Once you lean into the mountain, you can't get your skis going down the hill, which is of course the main objective. So instead of going down the hill, you turn your skis into the hill (trying to go back up); it doesn't work, and you fall. I don't recommend this technique: it may take you a while to get down, you will become fatigued, and you will feel even more pressure when you notice your friends waiting at the bottom of the run.

What exactly is concentration? To *concentrate* is to think about the information that is relevant to your being able to complete a task. As we have already discussed, the concentration skills necessary to complete any task are the ability to narrow your focus of attention, the ability to take in a broad range of internal or external information, and the ability to combine these two skills according to the demands of the task. The following principles, which explain how we focus our thinking under pressure, are modifications of concepts developed by my friend and colleague Bob Nideffer, whom I mentioned in Chapter One. Several books (notably those by Nideffer) provide detailed accounts of these attention skills. See Appendix B for a list of these and other references.

Narrowing your focus of attention and shutting out all distractions is required for writing exams, hitting a tennis ball, or getting ready to ski a difficult run. People who are good at this skill can stick to their plan and not get distracted. Individuals who are ineffective are easily distracted and have problems completing tasks. Examples of well-known athletes who are good at this type of focus are Chris Evert in tennis and Greg Louganis in diving. The good news is that anyone can learn how to become more effective at narrowing. Suggestions for improving this skill are found in Chapter Six.

Broadening your focus of attention, or having an ability to scan a wide array of information, is required for such tasks as driving a car, skiing down a run under crowded conditions, knowing what is going on at a party, considering a lot of options before making a decision, or analyzing the mechanics of skiing technique.

Individuals who are good at scanning are athletes like basketball great Magic Johnson and Wayne Gretsky, whom some consider the best hockey player in history. These people know where all their teammates and opponents are at any time, where they are going, and what is going to happen. Managers, coaches, bridge players, and chess players are also good scanners. Individuals who are not confident in this skill avoid situations with a lot happening, and feel overloaded when there is a lot of information needing attention.

> To concentrate is to think about the information that is relevant to your being able to complete a task.

Skiing requires the seemingly contradictory abilities to narrow your focus to shut out distractions and also to take in broad sources of information. Let's look at an example: you get off the lift at the top of the mountain and take a look over the edge. You see an immediate ten-foot drop straight down, and then an incredibly steep run filled with huge moguls. A normal person would tend to direct his or her attention to fear of death. But smart skiers don't waste energy on fear: they focus on the task of getting down the mountain.

Narrowing your focus to the line you select will activate the skills you need to perform effectively. While you're skiing your run, you have to focus externally and avoid other skiers or dangerous conditions. If you focus on your internal fears, it's impossible to focus externally. This might cause you to miss an important cue and thereby crash.

The first thing you have to do is relax by narrowing your focus internally during the exhale phase of a deep breath. Then you need to scan (broadly and externally) the slope to determine a line, scan (narrowly and internally) to analyze what is required for skiing that line, and finally scan (narrowly and externally) to negotiate the first turn. If your concentration skill matches the demands of the task, you'll perform to the best of your ability. Oh, did I tell you? You have about two or three seconds to accomplish all this. Remember that you need to possess the basic motor skills of skiing in order for your concentration skill to pay off.

> Skiing requires the seemingly contradictory abilities to narrow your focus to shut out distractions and also to take in broad sources of information.

It's essential to have already learned the appropriate techniques required in the actual performance.

Controlling Your Mind

Distractions cause problems. You may ski the same slope twice on the same day, with the first run excellent and the second run a disaster. There are many sources of distractions, but quite often our emotions will be the cause. A stressor appears, such as a steep incline or intimidating moguls, and we get scared. Instead of focusing on what we need to do to ski the hill, we focus on the fear. Fear raises our anxiety level, and we then begin to respond to the increased anxiety.

What is anxiety? It is a psychological response of perceived fear or foreboding to a perceived stressor. In the case of intimidating moguls, fear might cause you to perceive the back side of the mogul as a cliff that would mean imminent death if you skied over it.

Perceptions of fear and foreboding (anxiety) cause mental and physical problems. Mentally, you narrow your concentration even more than normal, which activates the motor skills necessary to respond to the fears, and you increase your chances of being completely distracted from what you're trying to do. This perception is a little different for each person, because we each perceive stressors in our unique way.

A contrasting perception of the moguls might be that you would think, "Wow! Now I have a chance to practice turning on the down side of the mogul." Guess which approach would result in better skiing? The first approach focuses your concentration on fear, thereby increasing anxiety, which causes your attention to narrow in on the fear. The narrowed attention causes increased muscle tension, which results in a very slim chance of skiing the mogul without falling. The second approach would lead the skier to activate the ski performance skills needed to ski the moguls. Obviously, a smart skier would choose this second approach and become focused on task-relevant cues.

How we perceive stressors is determined not only by our ability to focus but, more important, by our unique personal characteristics. Sport psychologists are now trying to identify what these characteristics are. In the section that follows, we'll be looking at common problems that can affect each of the major personality types we discussed in Chapter One, and some possible interventions, or courses of action, for improved performance.

> If your concentration skill matches the demands of the task, you'll perform to the best of your ability.

There are many effective mental skills, but only some will be effective for you as a skier. The best mental skills are those that fit your individual needs and personality. I suggest you clearly understand your dominant personality characteristics, and identify which kinds of distractions you are prone to and as many interventions as possible. Keep written notes as you read through this chapter. By going through this procedure you should be able to locate the source of any concentration errors and have a means of correcting them. The interventions are described briefly in this chapter but are covered in more detail in Chapters Five and Six.

Personality and performance enjoy a very dynamic relationship. Although an individual may have personal characteristics that are similar to those of another, each person is unique in the distinct way in which all his or her characteristics fit together. Your task is to see how your dominant characteristics influence your perceptions of the skiing environment. In many cases you'll find that although these characteristics are responsible for much of your success, they also may become liabilities when you're under stress. As we have discussed, you become distracted when you experience stress. If you can accurately identify why you're getting stressed and what happens to you after you're stressed, you'll be able to select an intervention that will be effective.

In the sections that follow, read the descriptions of problems often associated with what you have determined to be your most dominant characteristic. If a particular problem seems like one you've had trouble with, the suggested intervention for that problem will be worth your careful consideration. You can, of course, also use interventions suggested for other personality characteristics and their associated problems if they seem well suited to you and your needs.

Once you've gone through these sections, you should be able to identify your most important concentration problem. Dedicate yourself to solving that one problem. If you try to work on more than one thing at a time, you will find it difficult to see progress and maintain your motivation.

We've described earlier what can happen when skiers lose their concentration. Either they don't have a clue as to what they need to be focusing their attention on (task-relevant cues), or they know what they should be doing but have been distracted and are unable to concentrate on the appropriate cues. If you haven't a clue about what you should be concentrating on to improve your skiing ability, you need to speak with an instructor or coach. If you get distracted and can't refocus even though you know what you are supposed to do, then you probably need to develop more knowledge and skill at controlling your emotions and regaining control.

There is a sequence to learning how to gain control over your mind when you are under pressure. First, learn what emotions distract you normally but not necessarily because of a lack of skill at relaxation. You can become distracted simply because of something an instructor, coach, or friend tells you about your skiing. For example, I was once watching skiers at the starting gate of a slalom race. The coaches situated on the course were communicating by walkie-talkies to other coaches and skiers at the start. One of the coaches on the run called up to warn that the skiers needed to watch out for the number six turn because it had become icy. Everyone near the starting gate heard this report. From the body language of the skiers at the start, it was obvious that this announcement had immediately put fear into their minds. Instead of focusing their attention on how to ski an icy turn, the skiers proceeded down the run and became tense at the number six turn. Because they were thinking of ice instead of *how to ski* ice, several skiers lost control on the turn. The coach would have been more effective when he reported the icy turn had he reminded the skiers that they needed to stay compact with edge control on number six. Simply put, the skiers were distracted by the ice. They did not have a problem with relaxation; they merely focused on the wrong cue, namely, looking for ice rather than lowering their center of gravity and concentrating on edge control through the turn.

Second, there are also many skiers who become too emotional and lose concentration because they can't attend to anything but the emotion. Such skiers need to learn a relaxation skill that will cut through the emotion and allow them to regain control of their attention so they can concentrate on task-relevant cues. If you possess the necessary skiing technique, know what the task-relevant cues are, and can control your emotions, you maximize your chances of having a successful ski run.

Improving Your Mental Performance

As you make your way through this section of the chapter, work to ensure that you've dealt with each of the following points.

1. Identify stressors that cause you to become distracted.

2. Determine if you need to learn how to control your emotions or if you need to learn how to improve your concentration skill. (If you have both problems, you should learn emotional control first.)

3. If you need to control your emotions, identify why the stressors cause you to become emotional. Chapter Five will provide some techniques for emotional control.

4. If you need to control your concentration, identify why the stressors cause you to focus inappropriately. Chapter Six provides some techniques for improving concentration control.

5. Identify the one best intervention that appeals to you personally and that will allow you to improve your ability to focus on task-relevant cues when under stress.

Be critical and flexible in your assessment. You may want to modify your initial ideas as you proceed through the personal characteristics. If after having gone through this section you are not confident about your decisions, talk with individuals who know you well. If they agree with what you're thinking, you're probably right. If they don't agree, go through the chapter again and evaluate your position critically. The big test, of course, is whether the intervention works. You'll learn more about yourself as you evaluate and apply the interventions.

> If you possess the necessary skiing technique, know what the task-relevant cues are, and can control your emotions, you maximize your chances of having a successful ski run.

List Person

If you start your day with a list and judge how successful you've been on a given day by how much you accomplished on your list, you may become anxious when there is too much going on that you can't plan for, and your list keeps getting sidetracked. This situation can be even more problematic if you have trouble sticking with an objective and have a high need to control your life and your environment. When things start to get out of control, you become anxious and then lose your focus.

A good skiing-related example of how this characteristic can lead to anxiety is if you've planned to ski certain runs and work on specific techniques, but your friends, family, or others interfere, and you start to get frustrated. The frustration can lead to irritation with the interfering individuals, and things can snowball and go downhill from there (no pun intended).

Another example might be the young competitive skier who has plans to work on one skill but whose coach decides another skill is more important. This can be a real problem if you also have a high need to control and a narrow focus of attention. In this case you start to get upset and then will not listen to what your coach is communicating. You lose from both ends, because you are neither accomplishing your goals nor benefiting from the expertise of your coach.

Possible interventions:

• The easiest way to handle this problem is to communicate with your kids, friends, coach, or whoever it is, and come to some agreement about how you're going to spend your time. This generally requires you to make an adjustment to your intended plans. If such an adjustment is not an alternative, go to the next suggestion.

• Once you start to get upset or let your emotions take control of the situation, you need to do something to regain control. The easiest way to do this is to use a relaxation technique. Many skiers have been told at some point in their life that they need to relax, because they seem too tense. They are told to relax and take a large breath. Depending on how upset they are, this usually either does not work or provides only a short break from frustration.

Effective relaxation skill normally requires considerable practice, yet it does not demand a huge amount of time, because you can practice in a wide variety of situations. While you're first learning this skill, you'll need a quiet place to practice, but very quickly you'll be able to relax in any situation that requires your attention under pressure.

Chapter Five describes relaxation techniques in more detail and provides suggestions for practice. Select whichever technique appeals most to you. I hasten to add that it's also important to know how relaxed you need to be. I once spoke with a World Cup skier who was given a relaxation tape by a psychologist. He used the tape on the lift to the starting gate. He said that he was so relaxed at the starting gate, he didn't give a damn what happened next. For optimal performance, each person needs to identify his or her optimal arousal level. Figure 4.1 illustrates this relationship between arousal and performance.

Arousal, or the amount of nervous activation in your body, is related to motor performance in a characteristic pattern. As you can see in Figure 4.1, performance generally improves as an individual's arousal

Figure 4.1
The Arousal-Performance Relationship

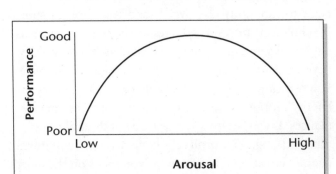

state increases to some optimal level. After that point, however, performance begins to decline. Motor performance specialists refer to this as the inverted-U relationship. It has serious ramifications for skiers.

Take a minute to think about a situation when you were skiing your best. With that memory in mind, try to assign a number to the level of excitement in your body at that time. Give yourself a 10 if you were "out of control" and a 1 if you were almost sleeping. The number you come up with will give you a relative assessment of your ideal state for skiing. For example, if you rated yourself at 8, you could say that you ski best when you're about 80 percent activated, or at 80 percent of your most aroused state. Remember, this is highly individual. What is right for you may not be right for anybody else. My friend Rick Frey, a sport psychologist, refers to athletes at the two extremes as chipmunks and hound dogs. Using Rick's terminology, if you perform best closer to the 10 side of the scale, you're a chipmunk. You probably have a lot of nervous energy and use it to power you to your best performances. If you're closer to the 1 side of the scale, you're a hound dog. You probably have a very low natural neural activation rate that helps you focus on the most important aspects of the motor tasks you perform.

Your ideal arousal level is also task specific, which means that different challenges may require different ideal arousal levels; in other words, the inverted-U shape on the chart will move horizontally depending on who is being observed and how difficult the task is. Some motor tasks require the hound dog approach and others need a chipmunk's energy.

If you are too relaxed and need to increase the level of tension in your body, you can practice a technique called *bracing*, which is holding a static muscular contraction for at least fifteen seconds. Bracing has the tendency to increase your arousal level. When you are skiing, just squeeze both your ski poles for fifteen seconds. If you don't perceive that you're aroused enough, simply repeat the process.

Let-It-Happen Person

You are a let-it-happen person if you live for challenges during the day. Life becomes boring if you don't have enough going on. There are at least two possible problems you may have if you are this type of individual. The first is that because you have a lot of energy, you tend to take on just a little too much. The second problem is that not enough is going on to keep you satisfied.

Possible intervention: You can probably reduce the anxiety caused by both of these problems if you engage in the realistic goal setting described in Chapter Two. If you're anxious while skiing and feel these problems are contributing to the anxiety, learning to relax would be an effective coping strategy. (Refer to Chapter Five.)

Social Whiz

If you know exactly how to act in any situation, the most common source of anxiety might come from interpersonal problems with others who don't share your social knowledge and skill. Others may perceive you as a "stuffed shirt."

Possible interventions: This is not usually a major problem and is easily solved by both parties' recognizing the right of the other person to his or her own personal identity. If you're on a team, you might be able to get the coach to act as a mediator. If problems still persist, hiring a team-building or communication expert would be an excellent alternative.

Socially Autonomous Character

If this characteristic is a dominant part of your personality, certain kinds of situations may be sources of anxiety that can interfere with your skiing. Because you don't necessarily recognize societal norms and rules, you may find yourself at odds with your friends, family, the mountain staff, ski area rules, ski patrol personnel, and so on. Most of the time common sense will guide your behavior; for one thing, you know you have to follow safety rules on the mountain or be kicked off. Also, your behavior may be too costly to your friends.

You need to be especially careful if there are additional influences that can exaggerate your own instincts. For example, you may respond to pressure from others by drinking excessively, taking drugs, or engaging in other socially deviant activities. You may act out of principle, or you may act foolishly simply because you have compromised your inhibition controls. If you're out of control you may very well make a decision that you and others have to pay for. Such decisions can also lead to aggressive behavior such as verbal abuse, physical abuse, or dangerous skiing that can put other skiers at risk. This is neither smart skiing nor smart living.

Possible interventions:

• The first part of the solution is to make yourself aware of prior experiences in which you made decisions that ended up causing you or others anxiety. Write down what you were thinking about and what you were feeling prior to your decision to act. In this way you can, first, identify what it was that caused you to make the decision and, second, determine your level of anxiety prior to your decision. If your decision was influenced by a high level of anxiety, it's possible that you can control your inclination to make harmful decisions by lowering your anxiety level. You'll find the relaxation techniques in Chapter Five helpful.

• If anxiety was not an issue, another way to analyze your thought patterns is to seek consultation with an educator or psychologist trained in information processing. It's possible to reorganize your thought patterns and decision making without changing your priorities.

Superperson

If this is your dominant characteristic, your biggest source of anxiety is likely to come from expecting too much from your skiing. You set high goals for yourself and have no doubt in your mind that you'll succeed. When success does not come, you may experience a feeling of loss of control, which further increases your anxiety and frustration. If another of your personal characteristics is slow decision making, it's possible that you can't get "out of your head" because of too much worrying. In this case you are likely to miss external task-relevant cues on the mountain.

Possible interventions:

• If your problems are caused by your failing to achieve performance goals because you do not have a clear understanding of exactly what you need to accomplish, the solution is for you to reevaluate your skiing. It's easy to set goals that are unrealistic, because you are used to succeeding and reaching difficult goals. This situation is a lot more common with high achievers who are just learning to ski, but it can also influence advanced skiers as well. Sit down and discuss what you're trying to accomplish with a person you respect who also knows skiing. The ideal person would be a ski instructor or coach. These professionals will know what you might be trying to skip in your skill development that might be retarding your progress. If you are an advanced skier, talking will usually suffice. If you are a beginning or intermediate skier, a lesson from a qualified instructor can really help.

• If you're a competitive skier, you really need to sit down with your coach and reestablish your goals. Ensure that you agree on what you are trying to get out of your skiing (that is, your most important skiing outcome), how you're going to achieve your outcome, and what you have to do to improve performance. Refer to Chapter Two on goal setting if this intervention appears to be right for you.

• If emotional control is not a problem after you have set effective goals, the issue then becomes one of achieving skill development quickly. The use of imagery can be very effective. Refer to Chapter Six for a complete discussion of imagery and imagery techniques. Remember, it takes a quarter of a second to perceive one signal and initiate a movement. Even at relatively slow speeds, your response will come too late. You must prepare yourself to respond in advance of the actual action. That is why you're taught early on to pick a line and then ski it. If you are forced to think while you're skiing, you are likely to fall, stop, or slow down. Imagery provides a method for you to ski a line without thinking. What you do is ski the run first in your own mind and then let yourself go. Pre-performance imagery programs your body by skiing the run in your mind. Your brain does not know the difference between the imagery and the actual event, so in effect you get a practice run. You'll find yourself picking your course but not actually thinking about how you do it. Imagery is not magical and can't provide you with skills and capacities you don't possess. The best imagery in the world will not work if you don't have the capacity and knowledge (skill) to carry out the task. On the other hand, imagery can help you achieve excellent performance of the skills and capacities you have. If you can ski moguls, imagery can help you perform better. If you can't ski moguls, you can use imagery to help you efficiently acquire that knowledge.

If used effectively, imagery is a beneficial tool. Research has not provided us with precise information about exactly why imagery works, but it has supported the use of this technique for learning, performance, and motivation. Anecdotal information from skiers and other competitive athletes also has shown that virtually all successful athletes use some form of imagery. The important thing to remember is to use imagery based on your capacity and skill level. For example, World Cup skiers use imagery before each run, and it helps them prepare to ski the run effectively. An intermediate skier on the same run would most likely crash, imagery or not. However, an intermediate skier could effectively use imagery to ski a run that was within his own skill and capacity.

You can employ imagery before you ski, while you're skiing, and after you finish skiing. The more you practice this skill, the more vivid your imagery becomes. Because you can control the events in the imagery, you should always have a successful performance in your mind's eye. The more knowledgeable you become about skiing, the more detailed your imagery can become. This mental skill is so useful for skiers that more detailed information about it is provided in Chapter Six.

Conservative-Cautious Person

Anxiety can also arise from being cautious or conservative. Being agreeable can make you a very pleasant person to be around, but people may end up taking advantage of you. You may keep going along with suggestions until you get mad and blow up. This can easily occur on the ski slopes. Just imagine getting yourself talked into skiing a run that you're not sure about. Your significant other takes you up to the top of the mountain, and you know you're about to die. The emotion that then erupts is not pretty to experience or watch. This emotion can not only make your run even more dangerous but ruin the rest of the day or the remainder of your ski trip. How do you turn this around and become a smart skier?

Another possible source of anxiety might come from inadequate skill or knowledge development. If you are cautious and conservative, you may tend to set safe goals and select ski runs that do not test your ability. This approach might not provide the challenge you need to continue learning. After a while it may seem that you haven't progressed as much as you know you could have.

Possible interventions:

• This first intervention applies to the conservative who prefers to be told what to do. This preference is not in the best interests of your mental health or your development as a skier. You need to take a more active role in planning your life and your skiing. The goal-setting guidelines described in Chapter Two are especially important for you. You will find making decisions a lot easier when you know more precisely what you're attempting to accomplish. For example, if you're a conservative who sets easily attainable goals, it might be a good idea to go at least one step further in challenging yourself. Don't argue with facts: if you've demonstrated skill and capacity, it's time to move on.

• If you're competitive, set high goals, and still prefer to be told what to do, you apparently want a scapegoat. It appears that you wait for another person to set your goals so that you can be absolved of responsibility if you fail. If you're conservative and also tend to be critical, you may not only avoid challenge but also blame yourself for doing so. These latter two complications indicate a need to restructure your thought processes so that you can interpret what is happening to you in a more rational manner. I say *rational* because it's not realistic to be continually critical of yourself and limit your achievements because of your thought patterns. The restructuring of your thought patterns is an intervention, called *cognitive restructuring,* that can most easily be accomplished with the help of a qualified counselor or psychologist. However, you can go a long way toward helping yourself by recognizing where doubts, criticism, or both interfere with your performance. You need to analyze what you think about before, during, and following performance. What you'll find is that whenever doubts creep into your mind, you'll be distracted from setting realistic, challenging goals and distracted during performance.

One method that has been effective in changing this pattern has been labeled *thought stopping*. As the name implies, thought stopping is a technique used to stop your current mode of thinking. Take thinking during a performance as an example. Put yourself in the position of looking at a relatively steep run with some difficult terrain changes. You immediately start questioning your ability to ski this slope. *Now:* yell at yourself (inside your head) to "stop," "clear," "center," or some other word that is personally important to you and associated with stopping all thought. That's the first step.

As soon as you've stopped thought, you need to do what sport psychologists call *centering,* which is focusing immediately on getting your body ready to perform. In other words, you replace body tension (which can interfere with performance) with physical readiness to perform. In this case the positive thoughts might be "Relax and flex your legs," "Keep your weight over your feet," "Remember to keep your center of gravity going downhill," and "Stay relaxed." These are examples of positive thoughts that are task relevant and that create the imagery and mental preparation you need to ski the slope. Again, remember that centering is a skill and needs to be practiced. Don't expect miracles, but if you practice thought stopping and centering, your thought patterns and performance will gradually improve.

Slow Decision Maker

Some of us have raised this characteristic to an art form. Unfortunately, it doesn't help us to get things done. Skiers with this as a dominant characteristic are continually worrying about their equipment, the snow and weather conditions, their own lack of ability, the expense of the trip, the cost of lunch at the lodge, the poor quality of staff working the mountain, whether their friends are having a good time, and so on. If you're a worrier, you can get so tied up in your head that you find it impossible to react to anything else and begin to miss essential task-relevant cues. Your performance suffers, and you get even more upset and less likely to turn your day around. Thoughts during actual performance might even be dangerous: "Don't get too close to that ledge" or "Those skiers are moving too damn slow, and there is going to be a collision if they don't watch out." Because our thoughts control our actions, this line of thinking can become a distinct liability.

In addition to suffering from mental interference, slow decision makers normally worry themselves into increased anxiety, which in turn limits their ability to focus attention on performance cues and enjoy what is happening in the moment. My friend Vince, who once had been caught in the rain skiing at Lake Tahoe, has a little of this characteristic. When I asked him if he wanted to go skiing, he got very agitated and said, "You want to go skiing? I'll tell you how to go skiing! Put on your ski clothes, go outside, and turn the garden hose on your head until you get absolutely soaked and cold. Then go inside and flush $20 bills down the toilet." Vince's skiing excursions have been somewhat limited since his Tahoe experience. He generated a negative perception of all skiing experiences from one outing. (It is possible to enjoy skiing in wet conditions if you are dressed properly.)

If you are a slow decision maker and you also have a strong critical tendency, you may turn your worry into negative thoughts and criticism about yourself. This combination can cause your arousal and anxiety to go past ideal performance limits.

Possible interventions:

• Goal setting. A well-organized ski trip will go a long way toward increasing your enjoyment of skiing. It's easy to worry when you don't know what will (or will not) happen. By properly planning your skiing, you take a lot of the worry away because you understand what is happening to you and what is going to occur in the future. A good analogy is studying. If you're worried about completing your term paper, you can't concentrate on studying for the final exam. The snowball of increased anxiety and decreased performance begins to roll. However, if you have your study schedule planned properly, you know that you've adequate time both to finish your paper and to study for the exam. With this worry gone, you are free to concentrate more effectively on what you're doing at that moment. You've removed a source of anxiety. In skiing, any time you remove a source of anxiety, you improve your performance.

• Relaxation. An excellent way to cope with negative thoughts is to use a relaxation technique (see Chapter Five). When you employ a relaxation skill while you are having a negative thought, you cut through the negativity like a knife and allow yourself to refocus your attention on task-relevant cues.

• Mood words. If you have confidence in your attention skills, an effective way to refocus your attention is to use mood words. Mood words are words that can alter your emotional state and focus your concentration. The best mood words are those selected from your own experience. Choosing a word is easier if you are an experienced skier because it's more likely you've already experienced a flow or peak experience in skiing. As you think back on such an experience, pick a word that describes how you felt and what you focused on. Some skiers have selected such words as *control, smooth, flow, oily, aggressive, power, relaxed, excitement, energetic,* and *coordinated.* The word needs to mean something to you and to describe your feelings during an ultimate skiing experience. If you can narrow your focus to the mood word, it will cut through the negativity the same way a relaxation skill does. It will also put you in an emotional state similar to that of the peak experience, which is exactly the state you need to be in to ski well.

This technique will not be effective if you don't have an excellent ability to narrow your focus of attention. If you have been confident taking exams or performing under pressure in athletics or other settings, you likely have this concentration skill. If not, you may need to spend time learning a relaxation skill, which you can in turn use to improve your ability to narrow your focus of attention. You can also trigger your relaxation technique with an appropriate mood word. Pretty soon all you need to do is think the cue word to get back under control and to optimize your arousal levels at the same time. That's smart skiing. Remember, as with other mental and physical skills, you need to keep practicing to maintain a high level of skill using mood words.

> Any time you remove a source of anxiety, you improve your skiing performance.

• Self-hypnosis. Another method for obtaining emotional control and effective concentration is self-hypnosis. Self-hypnosis combines a strong relaxation component with imagery experience. For skiers this is a powerful mental skill that can enhance performance.

You should learn self-hypnosis from a qualified hypnosis teacher. Most clinical psychologists and psychiatrists are experienced in teaching this skill. Although it is not essential for a self-hypnosis teacher to be a therapist, you should make sure that your instructor has had academic training to teach hypnosis, and understands skiing. There are some commercial tapes available, but I don't recommend them: it's important also to be educated about self-hypnosis while learning the skill. That way you'll not only learn the skill but be able to use it to your best advantage. Learning self-hypnosis exemplifies the importance of combining cognitive knowledge and motor skill to yield the best problem-solving ability. As is true for all mental skills, self-hypnosis can be applied to any appropriate situation in your life, not just skiing. Your ability to use mental skills is limited only by your creativity and your understanding of the skill.

Fast Decision Maker

Most skiing problems stemming from this characteristic are caused by your making decisions too quickly. If you are a beginner, you may take on too much, especially if you are also a superperson and have confidence in your concentration skills. You might find yourself in a dangerous situation because of your confidence and decision-making skill, the obvious example being that you might think you can ski a slope that you don't have the ability to ski. Or, as the saying goes, you bite off more than you can chew. This is not smart skiing, because you increase the likelihood of an accident. If you find yourself in this predicament, don't be squeamish about taking the safest route down the slope—perhaps sidestepping down dangerous areas and slowly working your way to the bottom of the mountain. You don't want to end your vacation or ski day early.

If you are an intermediate to advanced skier, be careful when you advise other skiers about their ability to negotiate a difficult run, even if you think they possess the skill. You'll have to be very specific about what they need to do to negotiate the run. The best way to handle the situation is to describe the run objectively and leave the decision to them.

Possible interventions: If you are a fast decision maker, the biggest favor you can do for yourself is to acknowledge this tendency and make allowances for it. Consult with your ski partners when making decisions about what runs to ski. Remember that you may have a great deal of confidence, but others may not. Your decision can affect others as well as yourself. In skiing it's wise to be objective about difficult or dangerous runs. The point to remember is that whenever you are going to make an important decision, take time to rethink your options and consult with others.

Silence Is Golden Person

This characteristic will not get you in much trouble while you are skiing. It's before and after skiing that keeping your own counsel may cause you anxiety. If you tend to be very critical of your own performance and don't seek out someone to discuss it with, your anxiety can build up. If you're also a slow decision maker and you direct most of the criticism against yourself, anxiety will likely interfere with your performance, because you'll show up on the mountain in a state of high anxiety, and it won't take much to push you past your optimal level of performance arousal (if you aren't past it to begin with). This problem will also be magnified if you're a person who prefers to be told what to do in skiing situations.

If you happen to be a member of a ski club or ski team, you might allow the tension to build up to the point that you explode, probably with anger. This display can cost you dearly in terms of your interpersonal relations with your coaches and other members of the club or team. It's smart to do something to avoid these types of problems.

Possible intervention: You might benefit most from some form of anxiety control. Any of the relaxation techniques will work. Having a coping mechanism will help your ski performance but will do little to solve the *source* of your anxiety. You will have to remove the problem by learning to express yourself before you blow up. In this way you can get your concerns out before they become major problems. Assertiveness training programs have been found to be effective in this area. These programs are available through extension courses at universities and night schools. Assertiveness training books are also available. If these suggestions are not effective, contact a sport psychologist or sport psychology consultant to help you work out a systematic intervention.

If you're a quiet person who generally interprets things in a positive way, your problem will come more from frustration or from feeling a loss of control when your performance doesn't meet your expectations. The frustration comes from your tendency to blow off poor performance, not from a lack of concern but rather because you assume you have to forget a lousy performance in order to get ready to perform again. The weakness in this approach is that you will not pick up on errors you are making and therefore will not progress. This situation can be very frustrating because you won't know how to correct your mistakes. If you have superperson characteristics, not meeting your own performance goals can be even more detrimental to your performance.

Possible interventions: If you're a member of a ski team, go to a coach, ask him or her to evaluate your performance, and get suggestions for improving your skills if necessary. If you don't have access to a coach, get a private or semiprivate lesson from a qualified ski instructor. Make sure you understand the errors you're making and have the instructor give you specific skills to practice to overcome any mistakes. Once you understand what you need to do, the anxiety caused by your frustration will disappear.

Highly Expressive Person

If you don't hesitate to express yourself and you're also critical, your skiing problems will come from interpersonal relationships. Your critical nature will actually help you become a better skier because you very carefully analyze what happens. However, you will experience increased anxiety and performance problems if you also tend to worry or to overlook the positives. You can become so critical of yourself that you obsess over negatives, thereby increasing your anxiety. And because you're expressing this negativity, you also have an impact on those around you. You'll become known as the cynic, even though you care a great deal. By expressing yourself, you're helping to relieve some of your emotions.

If you're expressive and generally positive, you probably find yourself cheering other people on. Although this is generally a positive characteristic, I do have a couple of cautions for you. If you're also highly competitive, you might get a little frustrated with performance problems if you're not being critical enough before you blow off a mistake. Also, because you're looking for positives, you might compliment another with the thought of giving encouragement and provide a positive reinforcement when it isn't appropriate. It is usually not smart to give false praise just to make another person feel better. The person receiving the feedback is likely to take your comment negatively. If the comment wasn't true and the receiver knows it, your comment becomes negative and you lose credibility. It's great to be positive, but sometimes you'll need to be critical, especially if the person to whom you're providing feedback is a critical-negative expressive person.

Possible interventions:

• If you tend to be hypercritical, an anxiety control skill such as any of the relaxation methods will help you cope with performance problems. You can also take some positive steps to reduce the effects of your critical tendencies. When you are analyzing your performance, evaluate what you did right first, then analyze what you did wrong. Integrate these two aspects by figuring out how to repeat the positive performance factors and reduce the negative. This provides more of a balance between criticism and positive evaluation, resulting in less personalizing and a more realistic appraisal of your performance. This simple procedure will also reduce any tendency to obsess over criticism. If this procedure does not work, I recommend that you contact a sport psychologist or sport psychology consultant to help you work out a systematic intervention.

- If you're experiencing performance problems and don't know what to do, seek the advice of an expert to help you locate the problem and solution.

- If you notice individuals responding negatively to your suggestions, you may be overloading with positive feedback. Try the following method: start with a positive, slip in the negative, and end with a positive. If you are generally critical and can't find a legitimate positive, it's better to keep quiet.

In the next chapter, we will look at how you can use mental skills to improve your emotional control during learning and performance.

5

Emotional Control and Smart Skiing

 Jane was getting her boots on at the lodge and thinking about her ski day. Her plan was to get a lesson and then spend the rest of the day learning to ski moguls. Jane had always admired the way expert skiers could ski them. They seemed to be able to adjust to any challenges. Her thoughts ran back to her previous attempts to ski moguls. Although she had no trouble keeping up with her family and friends on groomed runs, moguls were a different matter. She always ended up out of control after one turn; then she would fall back into the mountain as a means of self-preservation. Thinking about moguls, Jane's feelings were a mixture of fear and frustration. Fear because she was scared when she thought of moguls; frustration because she had always been physically able to do just about anything else she had ever tried. Jane was hopeful that the semiprivate lesson she would be

taking with her friend would be the beginning of a new and better experience with moguls.

The instructor asked them about their skiing ability and took them on a couple of runs. He said they skied well enough to tackle an advanced mogul run. At the top of the run the instructor explained that he wanted them to use their momentum on turns to take a little air, which would help them gain control to land on the next mogul and repeat the process. He demonstrated the technique on three or four moguls and asked Jane and her friend to follow. Jane's friend went first and did a pretty good job of duplicating the demonstration. Jane went into the first mogul and all her doubts and fears came flooding back to her. She did not time her weight shift well but did manage a turn with no air and little control. The instructor complimented her friend's effort and then began to explain to Jane how to adjust her technique to make the turn. Jane started to get annoyed because she understood what to do—she just knew that something was keeping her from doing it. The harder she tried, the more her skiing deteriorated. Jane then became angry at herself. When the lesson ended, the two skiers decided to try some free skiing on different mogul runs. By this time, Jane was having a tough time controlling her emotions.

On the lift Jane tried to analyze her frustration and anger. She thought to herself, "How can I expect to ski when I'm this upset?! I either have to control myself or go back down to the lodge for a while. Hell, skiing is supposed to be fun. I am just going to relax and let whatever happens, happen. If I fall, so what." Jane let her mind *drift back to the lesson, thinking about the demonstration and what the instructor had said.*

When Jane got off the lift, she stuck her hands through the ski pole straps and took off. She hit the first mogul, timed the turn just right, and was able to push off the back side. She landed with her edges in control, hit the next mogul, and was able to repeat the turn. Jane was thrilled. She realized that the only thing different now was her attitude prior to making the mogul turns. Her attitude was what was interfering with her ability to ski, nothing else. After this self-revelation, Jane made significant progress in her moguls skiing.

In Chapter Four we learned that good skiing, especially when under the pressure of new or difficult challenges, is dependent on our ability to control our emotions and our attention. This chapter is all about the first step: learning techniques to help us control our emotions.

Learning about your emotions and how to control them is an essential element in achieving performance excellence. Research evidence, anecdotal evidence from outstanding performers, and psychological theory all support the idea that each individual has an ideal level of arousal at which he or she performs best. Your emotional state influences your level of arousal. This relationship is one of the most important in any sport, and especially in skiing. When you are under or over your ideal arousal level, you suffer from concentration and possibly coordination problems. If your goal is to maximize your performance, whether in personal relationships, in the boardroom, or on the ski slopes,

> Your emotional state influences your level of arousal.

you'll need to identify your ideal arousal level, learn which emotions influence this level, and develop techniques that control it. The relationships between arousal, emotions, concentration, and performance are complex and not yet completely understood. However, evidence strongly suggests that it is our emotional states that cause interference in our ability to perform.

Any situation in life can bring about an emotional response. The same situation may cause one person to experience a positive emotional response, whereas another person may react with negative emotions. In Chapter One we talked about the importance of understanding your personal characteristics, because your personality affects how you interpret what is going on around you. Understanding your own personality can help you overcome interfering responses that are stimulated by what you perceive as stressful. Such insight can help you get control over irrational thinking that increases negative emotions. Although we won't be discussing ways to rid yourself permanently of distracting emotions, we will discuss coping methods that will control the negative effects of your emotional states. The good news is that if you can learn how to control your arousal level, you can control the negative effects of emotional states on your performance.

For skiing to be safe and fun you need to have your focus on skiing. The recent skiing deaths of Michael Kennedy and Sonny Bono are unfortunate examples of what can happen when one travels at high rates of speed and one's attention is distracted. You need to focus on skiing when you ski, not only to learn effectively and perform well but also to ski safely once you've achieved a high level of skill.

The first part of the sequence in learning how to control your emotions is to become aware of them. Emotional awareness is essential because you'll need to recognize the various emotions as *you* experience them. Cal Botterill, a well-known and successful sport psychologist, has made the point that experiencing emotions is a normal part of living, and hence we need to make sure that we learn how to use these emotions to help us perform. This includes ensuring that the emotions we experience don't *interfere* with our performance. Emotions such as fear and anger can be used to marshal your physical resources and concentration skills to achieve ultimate performance levels. On the other hand, they can also raise your arousal level to the point that your body tenses up and your mind goes into a state of total confusion.

Once you become aware of your emotional states, you need to identify the arousal level at which you achieve excellent performance; each person has his or her own ideal arousal level. Yuri Hanin, a Russian sport psychologist, has termed this area the *zone of optimal functioning* (ZOF). This ZOF or comfort zone is task specific, which means that you might have one comfort zone for skiing groomed runs and another for ungroomed runs. In California, our powder is often referred to as "California cement." It's a heavy, wet sort of powder that skiers must attack with technique and energy. Utah powder, on the other hand, has far less moisture in it. Skiing Utah's fluffy and light type of powder doesn't require the same amount of energy. An individual would need

> The good news is that if you can learn how to control your arousal level, you can control the negative effects of emotional states on your performance.

two different arousal levels to ski in these two distinct environments.

Once you've learned to identify your current emotional states and your situation-specific optimal arousal levels, the next step is to learn how to control your arousal so as to increase the likelihood of your achieving excellent performance. This is where relaxation skill comes into play. If you find that you often can't get rid of interfering stress due to fear and negative thinking, you will want to improve your arousal control skill by learning one of the relaxation techniques discussed later in this chapter.

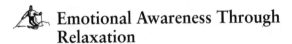 ## Emotional Awareness Through Relaxation

In any sport environment, we often experience sadness, anger, fear, happiness, frustration, and a variety of other emotions. These emotions affect our arousal system and, therefore, our ability to function mentally and physically. Most individuals are not aware of their emotions, even after their performance has been influenced by them. When emotions degrade performance, most individuals have no idea why their performance is suffering.

The first step in analyzing poor performance is to become aware of what emotions you're experiencing. Because the mind and body are parts of one system, often the easiest way to begin gaining emotional awareness is to use a relaxation method that combines breathing and progressive muscle relaxation. This method embodies the idea that your muscles mirror what is going on in your mind, and your mind mirrors what is going on in your muscles. We can use the computer analogy of hard wiring to understand this hookup between mind and body. Your mind is hard wired to your muscles, and vice versa. This relationship has been well demonstrated in experiments and clinical settings that have employed biofeedback. Biofeedback is a technique developed in psychology to explore the ability individuals have to control various biological systems (for example, heart rate and blood pressure). Using instruments that measure electrical activity in the body, researchers have demonstrated that many biological processes can be consciously controlled. When an individual has thoughts that produce anxiety, electrical activity (muscle tension) increases. What's interesting about this relative to skiing is that when individuals have a visual or auditory representation of the amount of tension in a muscle, they can voluntarily reduce the tension by willing the muscle to relax.

How can this information help you in skiing? By systematically reducing the amount of muscle tension in your body, you can enter a state of deep relaxation. Remember that when you reduce muscle tension in your body, you lower your arousal level; and, conversely, when you increase muscle tension in your body, you increase your arousal level. And because arousal is intimately related to performance, if you learn how to control arousal, you will have better control of your skiing performance.

Breathing is related to the relaxation response. It has been shown that a forceful exhalation of air results in reduced arousal. Can you see that the instruction to take a deep breath as a means of relaxing has some basis in fact? An added advantage of coordinating deep breathing with progressive muscle relaxation is that, as you become increasingly skilled at entering a deeply relaxed state, you can cue the feelings of relaxation simply by taking a deep breath. Suppose you became freaked out by a run: you could take a deep breath that would trigger a relaxation response; your mind would clear, which would allow you to concentrate on how you were going to ski the run.

There are two types of instructions for progressive muscle relaxation. In the first type you focus only on relaxing your muscles; in the second, you focus first on contracting the muscles, then on relaxing them. It's easier to become relaxed using the first technique, because you're attending only to the relaxation response. Using the second technique, the benefit of the contraction phase is that contraction allows you to experience different tension levels in your body, to contrast the feelings of relaxation with those of tension. Unfortunately, by attending to muscular contraction first, you increase anxiety, which can make it more difficult to become relaxed. I suggest that you try both methods and choose the one that works best for you.

The instructions for the two exercises that follow are focused on relaxation. To add muscular contractions to the exercises, simply hold a static muscle contraction for four or five seconds in each of the muscle groups you wish to relax. For the second exercise, I've added contraction instructions in brackets.

This first exercise is a way to begin learning how to relax. It's based on the idea that if you're in a relatively quiet area and not thinking about saying, hearing, or seeing anything, your mind will go blank. You can practice this technique sitting or lying down; it is an excellent skill to help you get a good night's sleep if you practice in bed before you intend to sleep.

Close your eyes. Start taking slow, deep breaths, and focus on exhaling. Relax all the muscles at the base of your tongue. You want to relax all the muscles associated with speech, so relax all those muscles deep in your throat and in your jaw. As these muscles relax, focus on relaxing the muscles at the back of your eyes that control eye movements. If you're in a sitting position, you'll feel more pressure on the seat of your pants as you become more and more relaxed. As your mind goes blank and your body relaxes, you may experience feeling "heavier" and "warmer."

The beauty of this exercise is that you can practice it anywhere, and, because it takes only a few minutes, you can practice it three or four times daily. Your skill will develop quickly with this much practice. After one or two weeks, move on to the second exercise. The second exercise will put you in touch with all the major muscle systems in your body, expanding your knowledge of your arousal and neuromuscular systems.

Someone can read these instructions to you, or you can make a tape recording and listen to the instructions in your own voice. Both methods work. If you make your own tape, use a calm, relaxed voice, and pause for a few seconds in the places that I've marked with ellipsis points.

Practice the second exercise in a quiet place without undue noise or distraction. You can be in a sitting position with your weight centered over your chair and your arms resting on your lap, or you can be lying down comfortably with your arms at your sides. Once you're in a comfortable position, begin by taking three deep breaths. Each breath should be a slow movement that feels as though air is filling the abdomen. Focus your attention on exhaling, feeling the lungs pushing the air forcefully, and your body becoming more centered. On the third exhale, focus your attention on the muscles of your fingers. Inhale slowly and deeply. [As you are inhaling, make a fist in both hands and hold this position tightly for five seconds. Notice the unpleasant feeling of tightness in these muscles.] As you're exhaling, relax all the muscles of your fingers and hands . . . [Tighten the muscles in your forearms and upper arms. Focus on this tension.] Extend the relaxation to your forearms and upper arms . . . more and more relaxed . . . [Contract the muscles of your scalp and eyes. Hold this for five seconds.] Next relax the muscles of your scalp and eyes . . . deeply relaxed . . . [Clench the muscles of your jaw and neck. Notice this tension and how it feels.] Focus relaxation down through the muscles of your face and jaw . . . Relax all the muscles in your neck . . . completely relaxed . . . [Tighten all the muscles in your chest and back. Hold this for five seconds.] The feeling of relaxation is now spreading down through your shoulders and chest . . . [Tighten the muscles of your abdomen and back; focus on the tension.] Gradually relax your abdomen and lower back . . . more and more relaxed . . . [Notice the difference between the feeling of being relaxed and the feeling of being tense. Now tense all the muscles in your legs and hold for five seconds. Notice the pain that begins as you hold these contractions.] Now relax your upper legs . . . down through your knees . . . completely and evenly relaxed . . . now down through your ankles, feet, and toes . . . deeply relaxed. Now go to any place in your body where tension still exists and relax that area . . . You're now in a deeply relaxed state that is very comfortable and safe.

Take a few seconds to enjoy the feeling of being relaxed. It's at this point that you can drop off to sleep, or employ imagery or mental practice to help you overcome performance problems.

Most individuals who use these relaxation instructions achieve immediate success in their ability to feel relaxed. However, being able to obtain the immediate benefits of being relaxed does not mean you are yet able to use this skill in every situation you encounter on the mountain. Remember, what you want to be able to do is relax under pressure. Learning to relax under pressure, like learning any other skill under pressure, normally takes considerable practice. Under normal circumstances, practicing relaxation procedures three or four times a day for two weeks will provide sufficient practice for you to begin applying the skill on the ski slopes. The more intense the pressure you put on yourself in skiing, the more skill you will need in order to apply the techniques successfully. You may progress quickly or slowly, but anyone can learn this skill with sufficient practice.

How can you judge your progress in developing the relaxation response skill? You'll need to have a way of judging your success on a session-by-session basis. Before beginning your practice session, rate yourself on a scale of 1 to 10, 1 meaning you're completely relaxed and 10 meaning you're totally wired. Write down your rating before you begin a practice session, and rate yourself again following your relaxation training. The difference between your pre- and postpractice rating is your estimate of how successful the session was. You'll notice that as you practice this skill you'll be able to enter a deeply relaxed state much more quickly. Pretty soon all you'll need to do is exhale forcefully, and you'll immediately experience the feeling of relaxation. When you can accomplish this you can progress to the next step.

Situation-Specific Optimal Arousal

When you can feel different tension levels in your body, and after you've learned to relax in a variety of situations, it's time to begin the second step in gaining control over your emotions, by evaluating your comfort zone for optimal performance. The easiest way to accomplish this goal is to begin by writing three stories. Describe in brief paragraphs what you were thinking about when you had your three best performances as a skier. If you're a beginner, use three experiences in another sport, in education, or in business when you performed extremely well under intense pressure. Limit your comments to what was going through your mind in each of the three situations. Then write three stories describing your thoughts during experiences when you choked—in other words, when things went from bad to worse.

After you've finished these six paragraphs, evaluate them. Estimate on a scale of 1 to 10 (10 for extremely activated and 1 for a coma state) where your arousal level was for your success stories prior to, during, and after each performance. Do the same for your horror stories.

First, look at the arousal numbers you assigned to the success stories. Is there a pattern? Are the numbers relatively low, mid-range, or high when you've had successful performances? Next, look at the arousal numbers for your negative performances. Again, is there a pattern? Comparing the arousal level of your success experiences and your horror stories can give you insight into your general arousal levels for each type of experience. The contrast will indicate whether you need to become more of a "hound dog" or more of a "chipmunk" to improve the consistency of your performance.

If you've taken the time to be detailed in the descriptions of your success and choking experiences, the statements can be very revealing in another way. In your success experiences, you can start to see, or confirm, what you need to be focused on to be successful in performance (usually the most important task-relevant cues). In your negative experiences, you can see what you need to avoid thinking about (usually fears and negative thoughts) to avoid interference or choking. Also, relate the cues that interfered with your thought processes back to your personality evaluation. You will note that the cues or stimuli that cause interference with good performance are those that you might expect from your assessment of your personal characteristics. You can use this same type of evaluation to go over other actual performance experiences, especially new ones as they occur. If the information you get is consistent, you're on the right track in determining what your general arousal level should be to improve the chances that you will perform well.

Having a clear sense of what arousal level you need for good performance will give you insight into how to adjust your arousal level to the situation. If you are like most people, whenever the task you face is new or difficult, your arousal automatically goes up. Likewise, whenever the task you are about to perform is well learned or relatively simple, your arousal decreases. This pattern tells you that in order for you to perform at your optimal level, you may need to increase arousal (perhaps by squeezing your ski poles, using internal statements that trigger activation, and so on), and in order to have a greater chance of success in difficult or new situations, you may need to decrease your arousal (using relaxation techniques, internal statements that produce a calming effect, and the like). Remember that even under well-learned physical conditions (for example, skiing on open, groomed runs), you may find yourself in a novel situation or difficult mental conditions (for example, being observed by someone who you believe is evaluating your performance). Being able, first, to detect the negative emotions that are triggered by such conditions and, second, to regulate the effects of such emotions, will affect how well you subsequently perform. Every situation you face in skiing will require some adjustment in your arousal level for you to perform optimally.

Arousal Control

The third and final step is learning how to manipulate your arousal levels under pressure. As we've already discussed, once you've achieved some skill at relaxing, you'll start to develop confidence in being able to apply this skill under stressful conditions. It's now time to integrate your relaxation skill training, your knowledge of each task-specific comfort zone, and your focus on task-relevant cues to begin to optimize your performance. The quickest way to achieve this integration is to employ imagery along with your relaxation skill. Imagery is covered in more detail in the next chapter, but the following example illustrates how these two mental skills can be coordinated into a learning sequence.

> Every situation you face in skiing will require some adjustment in your arousal level for you to perform optimally.

165

Let's assume that you get very nervous whenever other people are watching you ski, especially those who are closest to you. You've found that when you get nervous, you tighten up and can't concentrate on your skiing. In other words, being watched by family or friends triggers a stress response in you. The following script illustrates how you can begin to practice arousal and attention control. It's based on the skill and knowledge you now possess.

An Arousal Control Imagery Script

Imagine having a great morning of skiing on your favorite mountain. You are very pleased with yourself and looking forward to continuing your excellent performance the rest of the day. You just enter the lift line when a friend of yours skis to a stop next to you. You know how great you've been skiing, but as you ride the lift together, you start to have doubts about your ability to demonstrate your skill in front of your friend. On most of the previous occasions when you've had an audience, you've tightened up and not skied well.

The closer you get to the top of the slope, the more nervous you become. By the time you and your friend are ready to offload, you realize that you're too tense to ski well. Instead of looking forward to another great run, and focusing on sensations and thoughts that will help you have that great run, you can only think about what you shouldn't do. You become painfully aware that negative thinking and fear are dominating your attention. *[This is easy for you to recognize because you've been practic-*

ing how to become more aware of your emotions and what triggers them.] It's now time to get control of your mind. As you and your friend ski to the edge of the run, you take some deep breaths, and you feel the relaxation spread throughout your body. *[You regain control of your mind by employing your relaxation skill.]*

Once positioned at the top of the run, you focus on the slope below you, determine the line you want, and note where you need to make your first turn. *[More relaxed, you can now attend to the most important task-relevant cues for a good performance.]* Before you begin to move down the hill, you realize you're a little too loose, so you squeeze your poles as hard as you can for a few seconds. *[You adjust your arousal level "up" to achieve your optimal arousal comfort zone.]*

As you feel energy filling your legs, you take off. You're aware only of the conditions as you approach them, automatically responding to the terrain and steepness of the slope. Before you know it, you're at the bottom, realizing that you just skied the way you usually do when you are alone. Then you see your friend coming down the same hill, perhaps having some technical problems. You feel good about your own performance, and can't wait for your next chance to repeat.

The more you go over this positive imagery script in your head, the more confidence you'll gain for your actual performance on the mountain. This "success in your head" naturally stimulates a need to try it out for real. However, only practice makes for consistency, so mentally practice some more. Performing this routine repeatedly in a quiet environment is easier than doing it on the mountain. Eventually, you will be able to run this script anywhere you need it, including on the ski lift or on the mountain itself. (Most ski-related mental problems occur on the way up the lift or gondola, or at the top of the run.) When you've rehearsed in quiet environments until the script runs off easily whenever you want it to, try it out on the mountain. This procedure can be applied to any situation, especially races and when you are using more difficult skiing skills. Once you learn emotional control and concentration skills, you give yourself a chance to ski to the best of your ability. Because little, if any, thinking is required once you begin a run, you'll experience a real sense of flow with the mountain. You'll find out how amazingly your body can perform if you just give it a chance.

Applying mental skills to your most obvious emotional control problems is rewarding and fun, because you'll make great initial strides in your skiing performance. Remember, however, that this is just the beginning of your mental training. As you continue to challenge yourself with more difficult terrain, you'll encounter new challenges and stressors you haven't planned on. As you attempt to deal with these stressors, you may or may not be able to make correct adjustments while on the mountain. Return to mental practice in quieter surroundings with a new script designed to help you focus on the task-relevant cues. Eventually you'll have the confidence to practice both mentally and physically right on the mountain.

The greater the understanding you have of yourself, the more adjustments you'll be able to make both mentally and physically. The more success you have in do-

> Once you learn emotional control and concentration skills, you give yourself a chance to ski to the best of your ability.

ing so, the more confident you will become in continuing to practice mentally and physically. But how do you track your successes? It's important for you to evaluate your performance when you apply your mental skills to skiing. If you have a way of evaluating what you're doing, it can provide a good record of your achievement and skill development. I recommend that you develop a checklist like the one in Figure 5.1 and adapt it to your own needs and objectives.

Alternative Emotional Control Techniques

If you follow the three steps previously described—develop an awareness of your emotions and what triggers them, identify how specific tasks require different zones of optimal arousal, and learn to adjust arousal to

Figure 5.1
Checklist for Emotional Performance States in Skiing

I skied really well	1 2 3 4 5 6 7	I skied poorly
I was able to concentrate on the lift	1 2 3 4 5 6 7	I was nervous on the lift, had trouble concentrating
I was able to concentrate at top of the run	1 2 3 4 5 6 7	I was nervous at top of run, couldn't get the line
I felt confident on the lift	1 2 3 4 5 6 7	I had doubts about skiing this run
I felt confident at the top of the run	1 2 3 4 5 6 7	Slope looked too steep and difficult
Muscles were relaxed during the run	1 2 3 4 5 6 7	Muscles were not responding well during the run
Decision making was automated	1 2 3 4 5 6 7	Decision making was late, causing slower and poor responses
Skiing was effortless	1 2 3 4 5 6 7	I felt tired and exhausted during and following the run
Energy level was high	1 2 3 4 5 6 7	I felt fatigued and tired

Source: Adapted by permission from Robert S. Weinberg and Daniel Gould, 1995 *Foundations of Sport and Exercise Psychology* (Champaign, IL: Human Kinetics Publishers), # 284.

find your own zone of optimal functioning—emotional control will follow. How you develop your emotional control program is limited only by your own needs, goals, and creativity. Any method you use to develop your arousal control skill can be as effective as any other. The important thing is to find a way to get in touch with your emotions and to control the negative aspects of them or use them positively to perform better.

Most athletes have very good relaxation skills— they just aren't aware that they possess them. If you've been able to perform under pressure taking exams, performing other sports, or achieving in business, you possess relaxation skill. The trick is to be able to tap into your skill. The basic principle behind relaxation is that you learn how to focus your attention on a neutral stimulus such as a muscle, breath, mantra, EMG recording (in the case of biofeedback), or feelings of warmth. When you're focused on a neutral stimulus, you can't focus on whatever is causing you emotional discomfort, and your arousal level is consequently lowered. When your arousal level is lowered into your own comfort zone, you gain control over where you wish to focus your attention. In other words, you regain control of your mind.(For a more detailed description of the relaxation process and other methods for regulating arousal, see Williams & Harris, 1998, or Weinberg and Gould, 1995, both listed in Appendix B.)

Biofeedback

If you have a high need for control, biofeedback could be an effective strategy for you. Using this procedure, you choose from a number of ways in which you can see or hear the arousal response in your muscles. You learn to relax specific muscles or muscle groups by intentionally controlling the feedback you see or hear.

The advantage of this very effective technique is that you can learn to control specific muscles. Muscles such as the trapezius and the triceps are good indicators of general body tension, and they become tense when you are under pressure. Biofeedback training can help you control the tension in these and other muscle groups in which you have a known overactivation state.

The limitation with biofeedback training is the need for specialized equipment and a qualified individual to evaluate your responses. If this method appeals to you, however, I recommend that you try it. Simply call a local psychologist and ask for the name of the individual most qualified in biofeedback.

Autogenic Training

Another method that has been popular with athletes is autogenic training. Autogenic training is similar to progressive muscle relaxation but has you focus on feelings of warmth and heaviness instead of muscle relaxation.

Williams and Harris (1998) provide detailed instructions (see Appendix B).

Self-Hypnosis

Another method that is well suited for individuals with a high need for control is self-hypnosis. This method is very effective for reaching a deep state of relaxation and total control of the mind. As a matter of fact, regardless of your personality tendencies, if you have any trouble becoming skilled at relaxation using a mind-to-muscle method I suggest that you learn self-hypnosis. A natural part of this procedure is that you learn how to use imagery as part of the arousal control skill.

You should learn this technique only from a qualified individual; ask prospective instructors what academic classes on hypnosis they have taken or what certification they have received. Using hypnosis is a normal part of the training of licensed psychologists. You may find a sport psychologist who can teach you self-hypnosis or provide you an excellent referral in your area.

Meditation

Others prefer a more contemplative approach to learning how to relax, such as meditation. This technique might be part of a philosophical approach to living. It's also a part of many forms of martial arts training.

Mood Words

A quick and easy way to tap into previously developed relaxation skill is to use mood words (also discussed in Chapter Four in the section on interventions for slow decision makers). Such words need to have a particular meaning for you. A mood word can help you adjust your arousal to optimal levels and focus your attention on task-relevant cues. Examples of mood words related to arousal levels are *relaxed, calm, energized, cool, steady,* and *powerful.* Some mood words related to concentration are *focused, clear, control,* and *organized.* These are only examples to get you going. Review the success stories you wrote earlier and come up with a word that describes your comfort zone. The next time you feel yourself getting out of control, start concentrating on the mood word you've chosen. If you possess the relaxation skill, you'll be able to enter your comfort zone by concentrating on your mood word. Once you've entered your comfort zone, you can then turn your attention to the mood word that describes your best concentration. This helps direct your concentration to the appropriate task-relevant cues. I have sometimes been able to think "relax the legs" during mogul runs and been pleasantly surprised by an automated performance run down difficult moguls. The key word here is *sometimes,* because I don't practice this enough. The use of mood words is just like the other mental skills: the technique needs to be used as part of your skiing runs whenever it is appropriate. Practicing mental skills is an essential part of developing smart concentration skills. As we discussed in Chapter Four, the act of recognizing the effects of negative thinking— the stress response—and replacing negative thoughts with positive mood words is referred to by sport psychologists as *thought stopping* or *centering*. Thought stopping and centering are useful techniques for individuals who possess relaxation and concentration skills.

This chapter has discussed the ability to control emotions as an essential component of the critical mental skills required for performance under stress. In the next chapter we'll look at the second essential mental element: concentration skills.

6

Concentration Control for Smart Skiers

Carey, a fourteen-year-old junior ski competitor, was on the lift with her best friend, Sara. Carey was trying to concentrate on the forthcoming run and on what her coach had just told her, but Sara was talking so much she found it difficult to concentrate. When Sara realized that Carey was not paying total attention to her, she raised her voice and shoved her friend.

Carey focused her attention on Sara for the balance of the ride up the lift. By the time she got to the top, she was thoroughly confused about how to ski her run. After they got off the lift, Sara kept talking, even while Carey adjusted her boots. Suddenly, frustrated by her inability to do any mental rehearsal of the run she was about to make, Carey yelled at Sara to shut up, and took off for the start. She was still pretty upset when it was her turn to enter the starting gate. Carey was too slow coming out of the gate. She had a poor run, barely avoided a crash, and missed a gate. At the bottom she was near tears.

Her coaches had been keeping a close watch on Carey, because they knew something was interfering with her skiing performance. Her head coach had witnessed the blowup with Sara and had spoken with Sara. She figured out that Sara was interfering with Carey's pre-race preparation program. At her next race, Carey was instructed to ride the chair alone, to make sure she went over the race in her head, and to keep her attention clear and focused as she entered the starting gate. Without distractions, Carey was able to focus on task-relevant information and once again compete at her best.

Developing effective concentration skills is essential for performance. It's not enough to be mentally ready to perform: you also need to know what to think about once you begin. In Chapter Five we looked at ways to control how you feel. In this chapter, we'll deal with what you're actually thinking about during performance. For the purposes of this discussion, we will define *concentration* as focusing your attention in a manner that results in maximum performance.

As you've gathered by now, your personal characteristics play a critical role in determining how you perceive what is happening to you when you ski—in determining whether your thoughts are based on logic or on internal fears and doubts. When logic guides your thinking, you can reduce or totally remove negative emotional responses. The process of organizing your thoughts in a more objective way is called *cognitive restructuring*. This chapter provides suggestions for helping you with effective cognitive restructuring.

As we've discussed previously, skiing happens at such a high rate of speed that you really can't process information fast enough to be able to use it while you're skiing; most of your thinking has to be done prior to the actual ski run. Anecdotal evidence from skiers illustrates this point. After an incredible run, skiers repeatedly report that they did not think about anything; they just let it happen. Although this can't be entirely true—they had to avoid obstacles and negotiate moguls or terrain changes during the run—the adjustments they made were likely initiated well in advance. Racers report skiing two gates ahead of their actual place on the course. As a recreational skier, you have to be a couple of moguls ahead too. The most helpful mental skill for this type of concentration task is the use of imagery. Imagery can be incredibly helpful in cognitive restructuring.

> Your personal characteristics determine whether your thoughts are based on logic or on internal fears and doubts.

Internal and External Imagery

Before we begin, let's clear up confusion about the use of imagery as opposed to mental practice, mental rehearsal, and visualization. Mental practice and mental rehearsal refer to a specific use of imagery to actually practice performing a skill or event. The applications of imagery are much broader. For example, you could use the image of a pleasant and safe place as a way to relax, with no thought of practice. Visualization refers to the use of visual images created in your mind to picture a setting, event, or experience. For the purposes of our discussion, *imagery* is any image you create in your head. This image can represent whatever you're thinking about, be it emotions, motor skills, or warm, pleasant beaches. There are two general types of imagery: external and internal.

In external imagery you view yourself perform from outside your body, as though you are watching someone perform on TV or video. An example would be imagining yourself skiing down a favorite run. You see yourself making great turns and flying down the mountain. You see yourself come to a sliding stop at the bottom. The perspective might be from behind yourself, either in a stationary position or moving along as you ski the run; or it might be from a forward perspective, in which you are ahead or downhill of yourself, again either in a stationary position or moving along as you ski.

When you use internal imagery, on the other hand, you're actually in the image, experiencing what's happening. Rather than seeing yourself as another person might see you from outside your body, with internal imagery you experience things from inside your body. To contrast these two types of imagery, look at the following internal imagery script:

The wind bites into my face as it gusts over the top of the ridge. This is going to be an exciting run. I feel tension in my legs as I flex them to begin descent. I turn my skis downhill and feel the rush of speed building and the pressure on my skis as I initiate my first turn. I focus my eyes down the run as I automatically make my turns. My legs move with the mountain, but my upper body remains stable and facing downhill. Taking air off the moguls is fantastic, and I land in perfect control as I make my turns. A familiar and friendly pain begins in my thighs as I continue the run, and my speed builds. The wind pressure is much greater, and the cold is beginning to affect my fingers. I'm breathing in huge gulps of air as I come to a stop at the bottom.

Both types of imagery are useful in helping you improve your skiing. Generally speaking, the more skilled you become in skiing technique, the more useful internal imagery becomes. (It doesn't make sense to use an internal image when you probably don't have an accurate image in the first place.)

External imagery is essential for learning how to ski and for learning new techniques. If you can see a highly skilled skier performing the skill, you store the correct reference mechanism in your brain. This is the reference to which you will compare your future performance. As you begin to automate techniques, you can check various aspects of your performance using external imagery. The use of videotape is a good example of an aid that can help you develop external imagery of your performance. You can modify this image and your performance. The more you ski, the more vivid your internal imagery. The gradual shift to internal imagery will come naturally as your awareness increases and your ability with the new technique improves. The more you can relate to the image—the more vivid the image—the more useful internal imagery becomes.

Vividness refers to how detailed your image is. In general, the more senses your image includes, the more vivid the image. In the internal imagery script shown previously, emotions, vision, body temperature, proprioception, balance, and pain are all part of the scenario. Some athletes have been able to create such vivid images that they actually start sweating as they go through their performance. Vividness of imagery has been shown to correlate with enhanced performance. The more vivid the image, the greater the run.

A key characteristic of imagery is that you can control the outcome of your imagined scenario. If you're in control of your mind and you possess the skill to ski a run, you can then successfully ski the run in your mind. How does this work? At present there are only theoretical explanations; however, recent advances in brain mapping using noninvasive scanning techniques indicate that as far as the brain is concerned, there is no difference between the image and the actual experience. By using an image you're actually practicing (in your mind) what you're about to do on your skis. If you're able to see yourself skiing a run just before you physically ski it, you're preparing your body for what it is about to do. We know from electrophysiological measures that if you can anticipate what is going to happen, you have a quicker reaction time when the event actually occurs. You are ready with the skills to perform before you actually need them.

 ## Using Imagery

As you may have inferred from the background information, imagery can be employed in many ways to improve your skiing skills and increase your enjoyment of skiing. Let's look now at the four main areas to which imagery can be applied (summarized in Figure 6.1): motivation, learning, performance, and injury rehabilitation.

Motivation

Imagery can help you maintain a high level of motivation. When you have a clear understanding of what you want to create in your mind, you can better control your images. Suppose, for example, that you're trying to improve your mogul skiing, and you're having trouble

Figure 6.1
Uses of Imagery to Enhance Skiing Performance and Enjoyment

- Maintaining skiing motivation at high levels
- Learning new skiing skills
- Performing on more difficult terrain without error
- Enhancing injury rehabilitation and pain control

seeing yourself going over the top of a mogul rather than around it. Your trouble may be that you don't really understand why you *should* go over the top of a mogul. (The top of the mogul is often where the best snow is. Also, when you go over the top, less ski is in contact with the snow, which enables simpler turning; or the incline of the mogul allows you to take some air.) A

Imagery can help you maintain a high level of motivation.
---

clear and accurate image can result only from thorough understanding. That is why talking with expert teachers and coaches and reading can help you solve your skiing problems, both by improving your physical skiing and by increasing the clarity of your images. There is no place for failure in your imagery. If you're thinking about falling, you are likely to fall, because that is what your imagery is preparing your body to accomplish.

Consider the case of one young skier I worked with who reported with great excitement how he loved the speed of competitive skiing, but that he had one small problem: he kept crashing. When I asked him if he crashed a lot and if he thought about crashing a lot, he replied, "I think about it all the time, and I crash all the time. I just crashed before I came in." What he was doing was getting very good at crashing. He probably had developed great creativity in the way he thought about his crashes. I explained the influence of imagery

185

on performance and what could happen if he replaced his images of crashing with correct performance images. He never reappeared for the crashing problem. The point of this example is to be careful not to allow negative images into your imagery sessions, especially when you are at the top of a run. When you continually imagine yourself performing correctly, and you validate the imagery with your skiing, confidence will dominate your skiing attitude. And confidence is at the very heart of motivation.

Learning

Using imagery to help you learn is essential. Once you have the correct image of carving a turn, practice then becomes valuable, because when you ski, you compare what you've accomplished with what you had in your mind. The feedback you receive tells you the difference between your image and your performance. As your physical skill level increases, your ability to take in information by observing an expert model also increases—your imagery can include more information.

> When you continually imagine yourself performing correctly, and you validate the imagery with your skiing, confidence will dominate your skiing attitude.

A good example of this process would be your progression from the beginning to the intermediate performance level. As an intermediate skier, you will be able to negotiate longer and more difficult terrain, so your imagery should include more than the first turn. You should now be taking the first step in identifying a ski line and seeing yourself ski that line. As in your actual skiing, in your imagery you'll be able to see yourself ski a line sooner on an easier slope. As your knowledge and skill improve, so will your ability to create an image of you skiing more difficult lines.

> As your physical skill level increases, your ability to take in information by observing an expert model also increases.

Performance Enhancement

Using imagery for performance enhancement is a skill for more advanced recreational and competitive skiers. High performance skiing requires you to ski down a slope paying limited attention to what you're actually doing. Your main focus of attention is directed to the changing conditions as they appear before you. This skill is at the heart of skiing. Falls and mistakes occur when we let thinking get in the way of performing. Imagery is the best mental tool you can use to prepare your body for what you're about to do. Imagery is as essential to ultimate performance in skiing as your skiing technique and attitude are.

In competitive skiing you get only one chance to

walk the course. You can walk up or down one time. This inspection is intended to give you warnings about changes in turns, abrupt terrain changes, and variations in snow conditions. Skiers link these obstacles together to get an image of the challenges they must face on the run. They then use imagery to ski those challenges. Thus, for skilled performers the run has been skied mentally many times before the actual performance. If the skier allows doubts or negative images to interfere with this process, he or she increases the probability of making mistakes in the run. For competitors, effective concentration requires avoiding any distraction before, during, and after the run. Although the same principle holds for the advanced recreational skier, the recreational skier has the opportunity to ski the same run several times and make adjustments to imagery following a run.

> Imagery is the best mental tool you can use to prepare your body for what you're about to do.

Rehabilitation

Using imagery as an adjunct to medical treatment for skiing injuries is relatively new in Western countries. In sports medicine, imagery techniques have been found useful in assisting recovery from injury and in avoiding reinjury. This work followed from the use of imagery techniques in fighting diseases (such as cancer), in helping to control pain and bleeding, and in assisting post-surgical healing.

The procedures followed for using imagery in rehabilitation are similar to those used for high-level performance. The first step is to educate the patient about the anatomy and physiology of the injury; this knowledge enhances the injured person's ability to create and control clear, accurate images of the damaged area.

There are psychologists who specialize in teaching these imagery skills in medical settings. Call your local psychological association to find out who the experts are in your community. If you're fortunate and have injuries that don't require surgery, the same principles can be applied to your rehabilitation.

Assessing Your Imagery Skill

Before you attempt to use imagery as a skill to enhance one or more of the aforementioned ski-related areas, it's a good idea to see how effective your current imagery skill is. Your purpose is to find out how vivid your images are in the areas of sight, sound, kinesthesis (awareness of where you are in space), control, and arousal. Figure 6.2 provides a series of questions that can help you assess your imagery skills. These questions have been developed from extensive use in applied

Figure 6.2
Skiing Imagery Assessment

Put yourself in a quiet place where you will not be disturbed for at least ten minutes. Try to create images that use all your senses (that is, touch, taste, smell, hearing, and sight). Close your eyes, go back to your most recent ski trip, and think of your favorite or most memorable run.

First, just imagine yourself at the top of the run and recall the weather conditions, then begin to ski and complete the run. Then go back and do it again, this time including any friends or other skiers that were part of your run. Try to recall actual parts of the run that required specific turns or jumps, or moguls that were there. Remember how you felt when you got to the end of the run. Now, answer the following questions:

1. Were you able to see images of the weather, other skiers, or yourself?

No		Somewhat		Yes
1	2	3	4	5

2. Were you able to hear the sounds of other skiers or the sounds of your skis on the snow?

No		Somewhat		Yes
1	2	3	4	5

3. Were you able to sense your physical movements while skiing?

No		Somewhat		Yes
1	2	3	4	5

4. Were you able to control the images in your mind?

No		Somewhat		Yes
1	2	3	4	5

5. Were you able to feel the excitement or energy of your run?

No		Somewhat		Yes
1	2	3	4	5

Now add up your scores. The highest possible score is 25, and the lowest is 5. If you scored toward the high end of the scale, you are able to create clear and vivid images. If you scored toward the lower end of the scale, you will have to practice creating more vivid images. You can also use your score on individual questions to help you develop more effective images for that area.

sport psychology settings. Please read the instructions and answer the questions in Figure 6.2 now.

If your imagery assessment score is toward the high end of the 25-point scale (say, 16 points or higher), you have the ability to control vivid images in skiing. You should use imagery as much as possible. If your score was toward the low end of the scale (10 points or lower), you will need to practice imagery so that your images become more vivid and controllable. I recommend that you follow the guidelines for effective imagery training in Figure 6.3, even if your score on the assessment was as high as 15.

Figure 6.3
Summary of Guidelines for Effective Imagery Training

- When you are first practicing imagery, choose a place that is free of distractions.
- If you have trouble creating images, use videotapes or watch other skiers.
- Use a relaxation technique in conjunction with your imagery training.
- Be specific about what you are trying to improve in your imagery.
- If you experience errors in your images, correct them and run the imagery again immediately.
- Work at using all your senses.
- The better your imagery gets, the closer it will come to taking the same amount of time as the real thing.
- Take advantage of waiting periods by practicing imagery.

Effective Imagery Training

You may not be immediately successful at using imagery effectively to improve your ski performance, but don't worry about it: with enough physical and mental practice, anyone can gain control of vivid, performance-enhancing images. The guidelines in Figure 6.3 lead to effective imagery training.

1. When you are just learning to use imagery, don't stack the deck against yourself by trying to use imagery in a setting with a lot of distractions (for example, in a busy ski lodge). Pick a quiet and comfortable spot as free from interruptions as possible. After you develop more skill, you'll be able to use imagery almost anywhere, even during a run.

2. Use videotapes if you're having trouble creating images. Watch a sequence, then run it again in your mind. Start with small sequences and build up as you develop more confidence. You can do the same thing on the ski slope, watching other skiers.

3. Imagery is more vivid and controllable when you use it in conjunction with a relaxation technique. Research evidence supports this suggestion. Refer to the relaxation exercises described in Chapter Five.

4. Be specific about what you are trying to improve in your imagery. Are you working on technique? What technique? What exactly are you trying to improve? There is nothing wrong with re-creating a run just for

enjoyment. If the run was enjoyable, you must have been doing things right, so run it again.

5. If you experience errors in your images, correct them and run the imagery again immediately. If you find you can't correct the image, go to a book, coach, or instructor and find out how to make the correction. Then run your imagery again with the corrections.

> With enough physical and mental practice, anyone can gain control of vivid, performance-enhancing images.

6. Work at using all your senses. Skiing is a sensual sport with unique sights, sounds, and feelings. The visual field is often spectacular. There is nothing like the sound of skis on snow, and there is nothing like the feel of skis on about five inches of new light powder over a groomed run. The silence on a mountain is often deafening. The effortless moves of automated skills, like the sensation of speed under control, are accompanied by vivid and almost indescribable feelings.

7. The better your imagery gets, the closer it will come to taking the same amount of time as the real thing. If you are a racer, you can set your clock when you start and finish. If there is a difference between imagery time and actual skiing time, figure out why and make the adjustment in your imagery.

8. Take advantage of waiting periods by practicing imagery. While you are on the lift, check out the runs

and figure out where you might go. Then use imagery to see yourself completing the run or parts of the run. At the top, before you take off, is another time to get in some quick imagery. Waiting in lift lines is a good time to go over your previous run. If you made any errors, correct them in your imagery. In fact, you can use imagery during any down time: while waiting in a food line or riding the shuttle to the mountain, before you go to bed, or before you get up in the morning. As with any other skill, you get better with practice.

Attention Control Training

Imagery training can lead to more efficient and productive skiing experiences, but even imagery is controlled by what we are able to attend to. We have already discussed the importance of being able to attend to task-relevant cues both in learning how to ski and in reaching ultimate skiing performance. We will now look specifically at what is perhaps the single most important mental skill in skiing: attention control.

In Chapter One you assessed your ability in using two types of attention skills. The first skill is that of narrowing your focus of attention and not getting distracted. The second skill is that of being able to scan large amounts of information and come up with solutions. Scanning can be directed internally (inside your body), externally (out in the environment), or a combination. The attention demands of skiing require you to narrow your focus and not get distracted, scan both internally and externally, and switch back and forth between narrowing and scanning, sometimes with intense time demands.

Under normal circumstances we can usually focus our attention on the demands of a task. It is when arousal or anxiety levels get high enough to cause our attention focus to narrow that problems occur. (As long as we narrow on task-relevant cues, we're fine; however, this is not what most beginners do.) In addition to narrowing our attention when under stress, we tend to go with our dominant responses, which generally increases the potential for mental errors.

For example, suppose you are someone who can narrow effectively, and you are good at handling analytical kinds of tasks. What would you be likely to do if you were at the top of a ski slope and fear was causing your anxiety level to go above manageable levels? Your attention would begin to narrow, probably on one of your internal thoughts. If this thought was on the fear you were experiencing, your focus would become riveted on fear, causing even greater anxiety and more narrowing. Under such circumstances, it is highly unlikely that you would be able to focus externally on the ski line and start figuring out how to negotiate the hill. Your increased muscle tension caused by the anxiety, combined with your inability to focus on moguls or other terrain challenges, could cause delays in your responses, increasing your chances of crashing.

Consider another example of inappropriate narrowing. Suppose you are good at scanning the environment. You're at the top of the run, and you can't believe the size and steepness of the moguls below you. You narrow in on these moguls and develop serious doubts about your ability to ski the slope. The end result is the same as that in the previous example. In the first example, anxiety was caused by focusing on an internal cue; in the second, on an external cue. In both cases, mental training could result in improved performance.

As there is for other mental skills, there is a learning sequence for controlling your attention, and your skill will improve with practice. These steps are outlined in the sections that follow.

Educate Yourself

As a performer, you need to understand what your best attention ability really is. This may sound simple, but it actually requires some insight on your part. You may not realize that your abilities can be a source of problems when you are performing under stress. By understanding what your best ability is, you can predict the kinds of distractions that might cause your anxiety to increase beyond optimal levels.

For example, if your dominant attention style is to be analytical, you are likely to be distracted by an internal thought. The following are some examples of common distracting thoughts in skiing:

- I'm not a skilled skier.
- I'm afraid of moguls.
- Being on top of the mountain scares me.
- I'll never be able to ski diamond runs.
- I can't ski with my husband.
- Why can't I learn to ski as quickly as my sister?
- Why do I drink the night before I ski?
- I should have quit sooner yesterday.

You might be able to come up with a few of your own if you think about it. Look back at your horror stories and see what was going through your mind in those situations.

If your dominant style is to scan externally, the following examples may seem familiar to you.

- God, is she a great skier or what? I could never do that.
- This weather sucks. I have never been so cold in my life.
- Why don't those skiers watch where they're going?

- Look at that guy trying to carve turns.
- Where did she get that outfit?
- If I could afford those new parabolic skis, maybe I could turn properly.
- This slope is so steep, it's impossible to stop.
- It's a long way to the bottom.
- Take a look at that ice and those rocks.
- I thought this was a groomed run.

One of the easiest ways to avoid distraction is by avoiding the distractor. If you're afraid of moguls, don't ski moguls. If you get freaked out by being on the top of the mountain, don't look all the way down; focus your attention on the first section of your run. If you're having problems because of mental distractions, you can also keep a journal to help you record your thoughts. By studying the entries in your journal, you'll notice patterns emerging when you get distracted. Understanding these patterns will allow you to switch your thinking from the dominant pattern to the task-relevant cues that will allow you to ski well. If you have a tendency, such as being critical, that can cause an unacceptable increase in anxiety, being aware of that tendency will help you recognize early on when you're getting distracted. Once you know the task-relevant cues and what cues to avoid, you can proceed with success. Of course, this isn't possible for all skiers. For example, you may need to improve your attention skills or you may need to develop more emotional control before you can learn to focus effectively.

Develop Your Attention Skill

To develop your ability to control your attention, you will need to apply the goal-setting techniques described in Chapter Two. Determine what you need to learn, and set up a program for learning these skills one at a time. It's appropriate to work at developing attention skill if you have trouble processing information on a ski slope that would not normally be considered anxiety producing. Consider the following three attention skill improvements:

Improve Narrowing

If you have trouble maintaining your concentration and often get distracted while skiing, you may need to improve your ability to narrow. You can work on this one at home, or in any busy environment. Get a book or newspaper and put the timer on. Begin reading and, as soon as you feel your attention wander, stop the clock. Record the time you were able to stay on task. Take a couple of deep breaths, refocus your attention, and continue to read. You'll find that very quickly you'll increase the amount of concentrated time you spend on your reading. Pretty soon you'll be able to read with an orchestra playing.

You can apply this same skill to skiing. Determine

what you need to focus on to ski well. As soon as you get distracted, stop what you're doing, refocus, and continue. This skill is the easiest of the three to develop. Practice, practice, and more practice will result in better performance.

Improve Internal Scanning

If you aren't confident about your skill at thinking things through and making decisions, there are specific exercises that you can use for skiing. The first is to start writing down things that you have to accomplish in one day. The process of writing forces your mind to plan out your day. You can increase the amount of time you spend thinking and planning by gradually increasing content detail and the span of time you cover with your plan. Adapted to skiing, you might write down your plans for a ski trip. If you will be competing, write down what you expect to find at the race: snow conditions, number and quality of competitors, race strategy, and so on. Writing prepares you for what to expect, thereby avoiding many surprises that may or may not be pleasant. Gradually, you refine and improve the detail planning in your race strategy and start long-term planning.

This approach may be tough if you like surprises, but it will pay off in better skiing performance, especially when you start to pay attention to internal performance cues, such as being physically centered. If your center of gravity is kept over your feet with your legs and ankles flexed, you're in a position to respond instantly to challenges. If you're not centered, you are in a position of imbalance and will take longer responding to cues. You can't move your skis unless you're in position to move.

Improve External Scanning

This skill is important to work on if you have trouble driving on crowded freeways or skiing on busy slopes, or if you continually miss external performance cues, such as terrain or snow changes. The best way to develop this skill is by gradually adding environmental stressors. In skiing, using imagery is the easiest way to do this. Consider the following example. Let's suppose you get very nervous skiing with others on the same slope. In your mind's eye, create a scene with only one other skier, and watch her as she goes down the hill. You respond accordingly by choosing an alternative route down the mountain. Next, add two skiers and proceed until you're comfortable. Then double up, to four skiers. You'll gradually be able to view a large number of skiers, and, by judging their patterns and flow, you'll be able to determine your path to keep a clear line below you, slowing easily when appropriate. If this method appeals to you, review how to develop an imagery script.

Integrate Attention Control with Relaxation

When you know what is distracting you, but you still can't switch attention, learning a relaxation technique will give you a weapon to cut through the excessive anxiety or arousal and regain control of your attention. See Chapter Five for specific relaxation techniques. You can also use imagery if you've already developed that skill. You start with a stress-free image and gradually increase stress levels. Once you've learned to control your focus under stress in your imagery, you can expect to improve on the slopes.

The purpose of this book is to educate you about how individuals think and behave in a skiing environment. That understanding allows you to solve problems related to skiing. The following chapter provides concrete examples of how you can integrate the information on learning, motivation, concentration, and interventions into skiing performance.

7

Becoming
a Smart Skier

Robert was an outstanding skier. He had an excellent chance of making the U.S. development team after he graduated from high school the following year. Being out of school would be a big relief.
He'd been diagnosed with an attention deficit disorder in junior high school and had a tough time studying or paying attention in class. Because he had little confidence in his ability to do academic work, his success at skiing was a source of great satisfaction to him.

Some of his lack of confidence in academics carried over into skiing. He had most of his best races when he did not think of anything and just responded to the mountain. Robert's strength was speed, but at times he had to slow down to avoid disaster on runs. His coaches had tried to get him to use imagery to help him ski his line better and respond faster to race conditions. Because of his *academic experiences, however, he just didn't think he would be any good at imagery or other concentration skills.*

He'd recently had a great run, which his coaches had taped. As he watched the video, the racing experience came flooding back to him. He was barely looking at the monitor, and he actually felt the pressure and burning in his thighs near the end of the run. He hit the last gate perfectly and had maximum speed for the end of the race.

Later the coaches discussed the run with him. He had perfect recall of every inch of that race. After about half an hour of discussion, one of the coaches observed, "Robert, you have great recall of that race, and have an exceptionally accurate mental picture of the entire run. If you can do that, you can be successful at using imagery. Let's try it again and see how it works. This time we'll just start with the top of the race. As you get more confidence, we can gradually link the middle and bottom of the race to it."

Robert's first tendency was to doubt his ability, but as he thought things through he realized the coach was right. He had an incredible image of that race. Maybe he could learn to use imagery after all. "All right, I'll try," he said.

Within three months Robert was walking the course and using imagery to race the hill; his skiing consistency improved. His imagery skill with skiing had given him much more confidence in his ability to concentrate. He even thought that if the skiing didn't work out, he could always go back to school.

If you've studied the material presented thus far, you have some new tools to help you reach your potential as a skier. You may have figured out by now that almost all skiers, over months and years of skiing, are confronted with similar information out on the slopes. It's what we do with such information that determines what kind of a skier we'll be. Figure 7.1 illustrates the various stressors we encounter every day that we ski, and the positive and negative responses we typically make.

Every time you go skiing, you will face stressors. How you perceive each stressor determines your response to it. The response can be beneficial (high performance responses in Figure 7.1) or not (performance problem responses in the figure).

Figure 7.1

Positive and Negative Responses to Common Ski Stressors

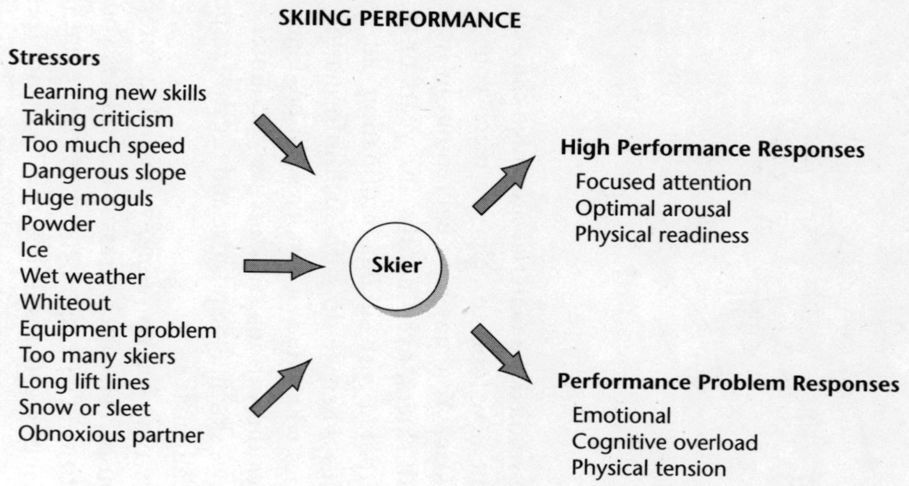

SKIING PERFORMANCE

Stressors

Learning new skills
Taking criticism
Too much speed
Dangerous slope
Huge moguls
Powder
Ice
Wet weather
Whiteout
Equipment problem
Too many skiers
Long lift lines
Snow or sleet
Obnoxious partner

Skier

High Performance Responses

Focused attention
Optimal arousal
Physical readiness

Performance Problem Responses

Emotional
Cognitive overload
Physical tension

The left side of Figure 7.1 lists some of the typical stressors to which skiers are exposed. One person might not give a second thought to, say, long lift lines. For another, however, the same stressor could result in an instant increase in anxiety, leading to distraction that can ruin performance. Whether the stressor will lead to a positive performance response or a performance problem is determined by your personality and attention skills. As explained in the figure, there are three kinds of responses that cause performance problems. The first is an emotional response. You might be experiencing anger or fear. These feelings can make you uncomfortable, increase your anxiety, and reduce your ability to focus on task-relevant cues when you are skiing. The second negative response is cognitive overload, such as thoughts of frustration or having too many things on your mind. This mental burden increases your chances of missing a task-relevant cue. The third factor, too much physical tension in your muscles, is caused by your arousal level being too high. This increased muscle tension can interfere with your ability to respond while skiing.

The most important factor in responding positively to stressors is to become aware of how you interpret them. You can then work on changing your thought patterns and controlling your emotions. For example, if you typically get upset and angry about long lift lines, you can deal with your response in two ways. The first is to avoid runs that ordinarily have long lines. This may mean skiing more difficult or less popular runs where there are fewer skiers. This cognitive solution avoids the stressor and will result in a more enjoyable skiing experience. If avoiding the lines is not an option, you will have to deal with the anger. A rational solution is to realize that the lift lines are going to be long and that if you allow yourself to get angry, it will spoil your day. The crowd is beyond your control; you can't do anything about the situation. Why not use the time in line to create imagery of the run you are about to ski (positive performance response)? You won't notice the time you spend on line so much, and you will be better prepared to enjoy a high performance run. This approach requires that you possess the emotional and mental skills to alter your focus. If they don't come naturally to you, you will have to learn a relaxation skill to gain control of your mind and focus your attention not on the distractor but on the performance response. Once you know that you can control your response to stressors, you'll know that no matter what happens to you on the mountain, you'll be able to perform to the best of your ability. That's confidence!

Checklist for Smart Skiers

You can use the following summary of the major points in this book as a guide to help you in your quest to become a smart skier. Figure 7.2 summarizes the checklist.

1. *Develop self-awareness.* Self-awareness comes first, because the greater your self-knowledge, the more powerful your motivational plan and the more effective your mental responses to emotional challenges. To achieve greater self-awareness, combine your own knowledge of your prior and current behaviors with objective assessments. An example of an objective assessment is the one you completed at the end of Chapter One. Obviously, a more accurate and detailed assessment is available through professional services offered by psychologists, counselors, and sport psychologists. No matter where you obtain your information, your assessment should

> Once you know that you can control your response to stressors, you'll know that no matter what happens to you on the mountain, you'll be able to perform to the best of your ability.

Figure 7.2
Checklist for Smart Skiers

- Develop self-awareness.
- Establish your skiing priorities.
- Develop your skiing knowledge base.
- Maximize your skiing potential through mental training.

show relative agreement between what your personal characteristics would predict and your actual behavior.

2. *Establish your skiing priorities.* Remember to establish your priorities based on your knowledge of self. Your strongest outcomes will be those that are most important to you personally. Keep this in mind as you progress through the goal-setting strategies discussed in Chapter Two, and remember that there is a reproducible goal-setting form in Appendix A.

3. *Develop your skiing knowledge base.* You can accomplish this important initial step in conjunction with the second guideline. You'll obtain the most satisfaction from learning specific skiing skills or techniques. Chapter Three outlines a systematic strategy for developing a strong skiing knowledge base.

As you develop skiing competence, or if you're an advanced skier, you can help yourself by improving your cognitive knowledge of skiing. A wealth of information about skiing is available through the Internet (including ski resort home pages) and at local and college libraries. A sample of suggested readings is provided in Appendix B. If the title you are looking for is not at your local library, it is probably available through an interlibrary loan program.

If you're a beginner, or if you need to improve a specific skill, look to readings that provide structured learning sequences. These learning sequences allow you to systematically learn skiing skills by focusing your attention on the first part of a sequence, automating that skill, then taking on the second part of the sequence, and so on. After you've developed your technique knowledge, start learning about applied scientific information from the sport sciences, such as sport psychology, exercise physiology, and athletic medicine. Many skiers gain a lot of satisfaction from cognitive learning.

4. *Maximize your skiing potential through mental training*. The top skiers in the world know that they must take advantage of their mental strengths and minimize or cope with their mental limitations if they are to maintain their position on the World Cup circuit. You can put the same knowledge to work for you. Chapters Five and Six explain how emotional and concentration control can help you realize your skiing potential.

Case Studies in Smart Skiing

The two examples that follow illustrate how individuals can overcome their stress response and not only improve their skiing but become happier and more fulfilled people. These individuals sought the advice of a sport psychology consultant to improve their performance. Following each case history is an analysis of what these skiers could have accomplished solely with the information in this book. I'm not suggesting that you will never need the advice of a professional; but considering that a primary goal of most sport psychology consultants and psychologists is to educate, you can accomplish a lot by educating yourself—by increasing your self-knowledge and your understanding of how you learn and how you perform under stress.

"Dawn"

Dawn, sixteen years old, was a member of a competitive junior alpine ski team. She was an excellent skier but recently had been having problems during and after her races. In her last race, Dawn had fallen halfway through her second run. In her frustration, she started screaming, yelling, and pounding the snow. When her coach came to see if she needed help, he was rewarded with a sound cussing out. Dawn's behavior was typical of many skiers who respond in a negative way to stress. This situation was pretty emotional for both Dawn and the coach, and Dawn was referred to a sport psychology consultant to help her out of this unacceptable state of affairs.

Up until the last few months, Dawn had been a very successful skier, one who the coaches thought could even develop into a world-class performer. When Dawn spoke with the consultant, she reported that she was extremely frustrated over her skiing performance and was considering quitting. After further discussion, she also revealed that she had been supplanted in the affections of one of the male team members by another female skier, who was now on center stage with the male skier and also skiing well beyond what anyone had expected of her. Dawn also reported that the coaches had told her she would have to make significant improvement in her skiing performance if she was to maintain any hope of making the U.S. development team. And because Dawn was older, the coaches assumed that she would continue in the leadership role on the team that had come to be expected of her.

Dawn was obviously feeling a great deal of stress in her current situation, stress that made it impossible for her to concentrate effectively during her ski performance. In addition, her responses to poor performance increased her overall state of anxiety.

Objective testing revealed that Dawn was extremely competitive and self-confident, and needed to be in control (thus fitting the superperson profile described in earlier chapters). She was also highly critical (tending to respond to situations with criticism and anger). Dawn was very confident in her internal scanning ability and therefore tended to narrow in and get distracted by negatives inside her head; in other words, she had an excellent ability to develop mental monsters. Dawn's high anxiety is unsurprising when we consider that she had lost control over both her most important relationship and her skiing performance. Dawn had developed a huge negative snowball of anxiety that was getting worse.

The intervention for Dawn had two objectives. The first was to explore the personal relationship problem to make sure that irrational thoughts were not guiding her thinking. The idea to convey was that relationships and distress over breaking up are normal parts of living and growing as a person. The second objective was to examine her skiing goals to make sure they were the same as those of her coaches. Was becoming a World Cup skier still her primary outcome in skiing? If not, then she could make considerable adjustments to her skiing performance expectations, which would instantly reduce the stress she perceived.

It turned out that Dawn had already figured out that the relationship with the male skier was over and not going anywhere. Her pride had suffered a blow, and this perception had caused her to get angry with her teammates and coaches. She acknowledged that her preoccupation with the relationship had negatively influenced her skiing performance. Dawn was quite willing to let the anger go and get back to having some fun skiing. She felt that she needed to do something to repair her current relationship with her coaches and teammates. She decided that when coaches and team members spoke with her, she would begin the conversation with a smile and respond positively toward them. (The consultant had already noticed that Dawn's smile was sunny and contagious.)

Dawn also revealed that a year earlier she had realized she did not want to make the sacrifices that she knew she would have to make in order to qualify for the U.S. development team. She had great experiences skiing up until it became evident to her that she did not want to continue competitive skiing much longer. Dawn also said that she wanted to further her education. She had shared none of these thoughts with her coaches or her family. Now she agreed that she would communicate her thoughts to them.

The results of these changes were quick and dynamic. Her relationship with her coaches changed overnight. The smiling really helped. The sources of her high stress disappeared, and her skiing performance returned to its original high level. She also gradually earned back the respect of her fellow team members and became an excellent leader and role model for the younger skiers, especially the young women on the team.

What if Dawn had not spoken with a consultant and only read Smart Skiing? Dawn would have discovered that she had a lot of confidence in her ability to handle analytical information and that she had the superperson profile and a tendency to be critical. Chapter Two would have helped her get her priorities straight and, as suggested, communicate these to her significant others. Chapter Four would have highlighted her skiing performance problems, and she would have discovered ways of changing negative perceptions to constructive perceptions. Because Dawn required no mental skill training, all she needed was to interpret her world in a manner that would improve her enjoyment and performance. Also, her improved self-awareness and self-knowledge would stay with her, increasing her chances of improved performance and satisfaction outside of skiing. Dawn would have come to discover that there is real opportunity for personal growth through self-education, no matter your age.

"Marie"

Marie was a twenty-eight-year-old mother of two who had just taken up skiing. Her husband, Mike, had been skiing for years and was an expert at it. Marie had been making slow progress in learning to ski, was frustrated with herself, and did not like it that her husband preferred to ski on his own while leaving her in instructional programs or on the green runs (for beginners). Marie had some doubts and anxiety because she had never excelled at sports, but she really wanted to be able to ski with Mike and other friends. Marie also felt that if she could learn to ski, she would have something she could share with her husband for a long time to come. With her time being more committed to her children and Mike heavily committed to a high-stress job, skiing could be an excellent activity for both of them. Marie sought the advice of a sport psychology consultant. She did so because she wanted to become a better skier; she knew that her attitude was interfering with her skiing performance but did not know what to do about it.

Objective testing revealed that Marie had most confidence with scanning external information and had little confidence with narrowing her attention under pressure. She had a lot of energy to accomplish things and was very competitive but had fairly low self-esteem and a tendency to depend on others for direction.

The consultant and Marie agreed that her problems with skiing were caused by three issues. First, she was looking only at the end result (being able to ski with Mike) and not at what she was going to accomplish tomorrow. This viewpoint resulted in thoughts that she wasn't improving, because she had no way of judging what she was learning. Second, Marie tended to take the constructive criticism of the instructors and Mike personally, which contributed to her anxiety and doubts that she could ever learn to ski decently. Third, everyone was giving her suggestions about how she could improve, causing her to feel overwhelmed.

The intervention consisted of one major change in the way Marie viewed her skiing experience: she had to take charge of and direct her own learning and ski experiences. This change required her to gain more knowledge about skiing, to identify what she could perform now, and to decide where she wanted to be. These efforts led to her learning several specific skills, one at a time and in a definite sequence. By learning in this organized way, she could feel comfortable in knowing that she would ultimately possess the skills she needed to ski with Mike. She also recognized that she was beginning to like skiing anyway, so it really did not matter if she skied with Mike or not; she would still enjoy the sport. Marie began a journal in which she recorded her goals, when she wanted to learn them, and what happened during each skiing experience. In this way she received constant positive feedback about her skiing ability.

Marie's second objective was to change the way she perceived information on the mountain and how she experienced performance problems. Because Marie experienced very high levels of anxiety while skiing, she decided to learn a relaxation skill to gain confidence in her ability to control her emotions. Because she was so good at external scanning, she often became distracted from her instruction, mainly by other skiers. Marie recognized that this limited her ability to capitalize on constructive criticism. She also agreed that she had to remind herself that the criticism was directed at helping her become a better skier, and to examine how she could use the suggestions in her skiing. These practices also helped her narrow her attention focus to the comments and not be quite so distracted. Marie felt that if she could control her anxiety, she would be able to focus effectively on constructive criticism.

Marie ended up becoming an accomplished skier. It took her three years, but she is now able to ski with anyone she chooses. Her family has a tremendous time skiing. In addition, she reported that once she started skiing the more challenging runs, she used her improved ability to narrow to avoid becoming overloaded with anxiety on steeper slopes and tough terrain. Marie still keeps a journal of her skiing goals, learning strategies, and accomplishments. She is now very much in charge of her life and, in addition to raising her two kids, has earned a college degree and is pursuing a professional career.

What if Marie had not spoken with a consultant and only read Smart Skiing? Marie would have determined from the assessment in Chapter One that her ability to scan externally might also be causing her to be distracted while learning. She also would have realized that she did not have confidence in her ability to narrow her attention. With increased self-knowledge, Marie would have a better understanding of how her personality affects her learning to be a good skier and accomplishing her major outcome. Chapters Two and Three would provide insight into why and how to set goals and how to set up a learning sequence in skiing. Chapters Three and Six would help Marie determine how to maximize her concentration skills—first, to help her learn to ski and, second, to help her maintain her concentration as the challenges from the mountain increased in difficulty. If Marie had taken the bull by the horns and initiated these steps, she would have gained a sense of control that easily could have had implications for her life outside of skiing. She would also likely have sought professional assistance to help her achieve her goals, considering that she tended to need direction. The best solution for her would have been to take charge, which *Smart Skiing* advises for individuals who habitually seek direction from others.

Postscript for Smart Skiers

In addition to the checklist for smart skiers that appeared earlier in this chapter, please accept these last personal recommendations for actualizing your potential to become a smarter skier tomorrow than you are today. Becoming a smart skier is a dynamic process, one that can and should be enjoyed. Good luck in your quest.

1. *Use critical thinking skills.* Integrate information from as many sources as possible when you are making decisions. You may nonetheless make incorrect decisions, and that's OK. Treat your decisions as hypotheses based on as much information as you can get your hands on. If subsequent objective information contradicts your hypothesis, you need only to evaluate

and make changes as necessary. Living is a dynamic process. The better your sources of information, and the more information you have, the more likely it is that you will make correct decisions. Just recall how your personality and your concentration skills can bias the way you perceive what is happening to you. The more you practice critical thinking skills, the more adept you become.

2. *Write things down.* Keeping a written record of your discoveries, outcomes, goals, objectives, and plans will pay large dividends as you proceed. I can't tell you how many athletes have reported that they worked out their initial problems, only to have others appear later on. By looking back at their writings, they were able to determine quickly what was happening to them and make appropriate adjustments. Having a record of your thinking allows you to take advantage of your previous learning.

3. *Be specific.* What is the major outcome you wish to achieve with your skiing? What performance levels do you need to achieve in order to reach your outcome? How many hours of effort are you going to put in to reach your performance goals? What are your attention strengths and weaknesses? What are your dominant personal characteristics? What distracts you from effective concentration? What causes you to become anxious? Exactly what can you do to avoid or cope with

distractions? How can you control anxiety? What should you do first? How will you accomplish it? How long is it going to take you? How is this going to improve your skiing? What happens when things don't go as planned?

4. *Take charge of your skiing.* Listen to others—teachers, coaches, significant others, professionals, and fellow skiers—but take their suggestions as information only, to be evaluated like any other piece of knowledge. If you know where you're headed, how you're going to get there, and why, interpreting information becomes easier. Your attention becomes more directed and focused. Taking charge of your life may be the fundamental component of psychological health. The stronger your psychological health, the more likely you will respond in a positive way to life's stressors.

5. *Have some fun.* The more you find out about yourself, the greater chance you have of making decisions that will result in personal satisfaction. If you love to compete, get involved in racing. If you enjoy learning, make sure you know how to improve your skiing. The better you understand yourself, the more you can turn life events your way. Each of us returns to skiing because it is satisfying. Knowing the source of your satisfaction is what makes you a smart skier and what keeps bringing you back to the mountains. Once again, good luck with your skiing, and I wish you continual enjoyment of it!

Appendix A: Goal-Setting Guidelines

Goal-Setting Worksheet

Outcome 1 _____

    Performance goal 1 _____
                    Effort:
                            Hours T _____
                            Hours I _____

    Performance goal 2 _____
                    Effort:
                            Hours T _____
                            Hours I _____

    Performance goal 3 _____
                    Effort:
                            Hours T _____
                            Hours I _____

T = training, I = instruction

Goal-Setting Worksheet

Outcome 2 _____

                    Performance goal 1 _____

                                   Effort:

                                          Hours T _____

                                          Hours I _____

                    Performance goal 2 _____

                                   Effort:

                                          Hours T _____

                                          Hours I _____

                    Performance goal 3 _____

                                   Effort:

                                          Hours T _____

                                          Hours I _____

T = training, I = instruction

Goal-Setting Worksheet

Outcome 3 _____

        Performance goal 1 _____

             Effort:

                Hours T _____

                Hours I _____

        Performance goal 2 _____

             Effort:

                Hours T _____

                Hours I _____

        Performance goal 3 _____

             Effort:

                Hours T _____

                Hours I _____

T = training, I = instruction

Appendix B: Selected Skiing References

Burnett, K. (1994). *Personal training organizer for alpine skiing*. Boise, ID: Sports Performance Systems.

Cox, R. H. (1994). *Sport psychology: Concepts and applications* (3rd ed.). Dubuque, IA: Brown and Benchmark.

Foster, E. P. (1996). *Skiing and the art of carving*. Harrisburg, VA: Turning Point Ski Foundation.

Greene, N. (1996). *Nancy Greene's pocket guide to skiing*. Sun Peaks, BC: Cahilty Lodge.

Loudis, L. A., Lobitz, C. W., & Singer, K. M. (1986). *Skiing out of your mind: The psychology of peak performance*. Champaign, IL: Leisure Press.

Nideffer, R. M. (1976). *The inner athlete*. Los Gatos, CA: Enhanced Performance Services.

Nideffer, R. M. (1984). *The ethics and practice of applied sport psychology*. Ithaca, NY: Mouvement Publications.

Nideffer, R. M., & Sagal, M. (1998). Concentration and attention control training. In J. Williams (Ed.), *Applied sport psychology*. Mountain View, CA: Mayfield.

Orlick, T. (1990). *In pursuit of excellence* (2nd ed.). Champaign, IL: Human Kinetics.

Patrick, T. (1987). *Six ways to reach your skiing potential*. Lanham, MD: Sports Illustrated Books.

Vealey, R. S., & Greenleaf, C. F. (1998). Seeing is believing: Understanding and using imagery in sport. In J. Williams (Ed.), *Applied sport psychology*. Mountain View, CA: Mayfield.

Weinberg, R. S., & Gould, D. (1995). *Foundations of sport and exercise psychology*. Champaign, IL: Human Kinetics.

Williams, J., & Harris, D. (1998). Relaxation and energizing techniques for regulation of arousal. In J. Williams (Ed.), *Applied sport psychology*. Mountain View, CA: Mayfield.

Yacenda, J., & Ross, T. (1998). *High-performance skiing*. Champaign, IL: Human Kinetics.

About the Author

Dennis J. Selder is a professor in the Department of Exercise and Nutritional Sciences at San Diego State University, where he teaches undergraduate and graduate students in sport psychology. He has also been a faculty member at the University of California at San Diego and an adjunct faculty member at California Professional School of Psychology. He has held his current position for thirty years and is the current graduate coordinator for sport psychology. In addition to teaching, Selder has published more than fifty research and theoretical articles in scientific journals. He has been active as a speaker around the world, having given papers in Italy, Spain, Australia, Singapore, and Portugal, as well as most major cities in Canada and the United States. He earned his bachelor's and master's degrees in physical education at the University of British Columbia, where he played varsity hockey and varsity basketball, and his Ph.D. at Ohio State University.

Selder has also been active as a sport psychology consultant, conducting workshops, providing individual and team consulting services, and supervising graduate students in their applied work. Clients have been athletes of all ages at all levels of performance, from young children to Olympic and professional athletes, in addition to members of organizations and teams. He has also provided consulting services to the U.S. Navy Seal Team training program in San Diego and served for eight years as the sport psychology consultant to the Mammoth Mountain Alpine Racing Team.

Selder has coached intercollegiate hockey teams at the University of British Columbia (1963) and Dalhousie University (1964–1966) and the club team at San Diego State University (1970–1976). He has been skiing since 1959 and also enjoys running, sailing, and golf.

About the
General Editor

Rick Frey has an impressive record in the physical activity field. A professor of kinesiology at San Diego State University (SDSU) in the 1970s, he was a racquetball teaching professional, weight loss coordinator, and health fitness leader at the prestigious Canyon Racquet Club in Salt Lake City, Utah, during the early 1980s, professor and chair of the Department of Physical Education at the University of Alaska, Anchorage (UAA), between 1982 and 1988, and director of the academic book division of Human Kinetics Publishers in Champaign, Illinois, between 1988 and 1996.

A thirty-year rugby veteran, he coached the sport at both the University of Alberta (UA) in Edmonton, Canada, and the University of Illinois (UI). He also coached wrestling (UA) and ice hockey (UAA) and served as the sport psychology consultant to numerous individual and team sport athletes at UAA, SDSU, and

UI for more than a dozen years. Athletes he has consulted with have gone on to earn All-American, professional, and Olympic honors.

Former president of the Alaska Association for Health, Physical Education, Recreation, and Dance, Frey has written more than thirty professional and scholarly articles and a book chapter and has given papers at more than fifty state, regional, and national conferences in the physical activity field.

With graduate degrees in sport psychology and human motor performance, he is currently an adjunct professor of kinesiology and outdoor recreation at the Eastern Sierra College Center of Cerro Coso Community College in Bishop, California, where he also serves more than 120 older adults as a senior exercise specialist for the Inyo County Office of Education. He is president and founder of AcquisitionServices, a publishing consulting firm in the exercise science field.

Index

233

125; expert, in ski resorts, 44; performance goal setting and, 44, 48, 52, 132. *See also* Instructors

Cognitive learning phase, 75–80, 210–211

Cognitive restructuring, 136–138, 175, 179. *See also* Attention control training; Imagery

Competition: imagery used for, 187–188; performance under, 111–112; as possible outcome, 43–44; resources about, 56. *See also* Racers

Competitive drive, 30–31; socialization and, 35–36

Concentration skills: assessment of, 14, 17–18; attention control training for, 194–202; and decision making, 8, 12–14; defined, 115; dimensions of attention and, 12–13; imagery techniques for, 180–194; learning, 96; and learning, 13–14, 83–84; and perception of stressors, 14–16; and performance, 12, 109, 113–117, 121, 123, 178–180; for performance under pressure, 113–117, 123–148; problems in, of intermediate skiers, 104. *See also* Attention control training; Attention focus; Imagery; Mental skills

Conditions. *See* Practice conditions; Snow; Terrain; Weather

Control, need for, 33; frustration and, 145–146; and learning, 86; and performance goal setting, 48. *See also* Direction, preference for

Course, walking the, 187–188

Cox, R. H., 51, 227

Crashing, imagery and, 185–186

Critical feedback acceptance: self-confidence and, 32–33, 84–85; truthfulness and, 147

Critical persons, 33–34; in case study, 212–215; expressive, 22, 147–148; list-person, 49; mental techniques for, 136–138; performance goal setting for, 47–48, 49; and positive feedback, 85; silent, 22, 144; slow decision-maker, 139; superperson, 47–48, 215

Critical thinking skills, 219–220

Cues, learning, 14, 100. *See also* Attention focus; External attention focus; Internal attention focus

D

"Dawn" case study, 212–215

Decision making: concentration and, 12–14; critical thinking skills for, 219–220; personal characteristics and, 11–12; personality and, 8–16; personality core and, 8–10,